Time Alchemy:
A Dynamic and Soulful Approach
to Managing Your Time

by Ulrika Brättemark

*May you find a deep sense
of meaning in each moment*

Table of Contents

Note from the Author

Full disclosure . . . I have never hit rock bottom. I have never had a near-death experience. I have never had my marital rug pulled out from under me. Nor have I ever had to choose between putting food on the table or getting my kids to the doctor.

I believe it is possible—and I am actively working to prove this in my own life—that we can each "wake up" and find our mission, without the occurrence of dramatic or extremely life-changing events. I believe it is possible to take charge of our lives right now, one deliberate choice at a time, without first getting "whacked in the head" by a drastic life-changing event. For those who have a clear personal mission as a result of a tragic event, I am happy that you were able to turn those circumstances into something useful. For those of us fortunate enough not to have been severely whacked over the head by drastic life events, it can actually be harder to find and pursue a particular cause. It requires us to make more deliberate choices and find our inner drive because there's seemingly no urgency. Yet, each decision we make in each present moment adds up to how we end up living our lives and what defines our life journey. If we courageously claim the driver seat of our lives and don't default to what others expect of us, we can significantly impact the world in this lifetime.

I believe I'm here to enable an increased positive impact in the world. I think that each and every one of us is here to leverage our life experience, skill, and energy to do as much good as we can in the world. I feel incredibly grateful for my "first-world problems" and am committed to using this privileged position to show up to, directly or indirectly, support others who want to have a positive impact on the world.

I draw from my multiple-decade experience at a large software company as a diligently organized business analyst turned playful and dynamic agile coach. My time in those roles provided me with skills related to structure as well as flexibility. Having lived and worked in multiple countries, I've become both culture- and business-savvy, learned how to lead deep and dynamic teamwork, and dealt with the complexity of large-system implementations. Add to that my explorations as a curious, expressive arts practitioner, years of moonlighting as a yoga teacher, and this most recent why-not-give-it-a-go at authorship, and the whole picture is emerging. I apply all that I teach to my own life, in the very dynamic adventures of motherhood, the multifaceted world of group facilitation, and all the hats I get to wear as a solopreneur.

I have a passion for finding win-win-win situations, and I thrive when I can support others in finding their unique contribution to this wonderfully wild world of ours. Our contributions can simultaneously benefit those we serve directly, give us a sense of personal fulfillment, and positively contribute to the world at large.

Visual:

- Inner circle - personal fulfillment
- Middle circle - direct service/impact
- Outside of circles - impact on the world at large

One of my superpowers is to take big theoretical concepts and make them practically applicable in our daily lives, marrying philosophy with pragmatism. I am intrigued by exploring different sources of wisdom and ways to make them relevant in our daily lives. I hope that through my writing you consider the conceptual ideas that I'm sharing, but most of all, I hope you implement them in your life in a meaningful way. I wish for you to find time management practices that truly support you, not just in the moment but on your lifelong journey, leading to a truly rich experience of life.

Don't Take My Word for It

I recently read a book about how to empower myself and truly feel like I'm living MY life. It was one big pep talk. For most of the book I felt yelled at; You HAVE to do this! NEVER do that! Own it! Claim it! Don't let anyone or anything get in your way! The author apparently has a very successful business and although I assume her intentions were good, the emphasis on just how big and successful her company was took up almost half of the book. The book left me with no additional tools or inspiration to actually pursue my goals.

Although I want to share some personal stories of both trials and successes and what I have learned from experience, my intention in doing so is so that you feel inspired to try something. Apply it to your situation. Test it out and find out for yourself. Let your time management approach be as alive and unique as you are.

I have worked with clients from diverse situations and backgrounds, and the tools and techniques I suggest have been proven successful many times over. I will share some of those stories too, as it might help you relate and better understand the approach. After all, only you can empower and motivate you. I hope my stories will inspire you to inquire within yourself and discover how to do so.

We need to continuously inquire within to find our own truth. It takes work, throughout our lifetime, but in the end, we each get to more fully assert that we truly lived our life.

People come to me wanting help with how they can do more with their time. But when I talk to them further, it becomes clear they really want to do less of what they don't care much about and more of what is deeply meaningful to them. They want a richer experience of time and of life. A powerful way to do that is to regularly ask ourselves what our values and intentions are, and then make our everyday choices of how we spend our time based on those priorities, experimenting our way to a more fulfilling daily life.

The approach is simple yet profound and, oh, so rewarding. Remember that most significant changes happen a step at a time. I wish you inspiration and balance on a daily basis. I want to support you in creating an everyday existence in which you feel truly alive.

Introduction

To manage our time well we need to be deliberate about how we spend our days based on our dreams, goals, and values. That's it.

So, why did I write a whole book about it?

Well, because we are complicated beings living in a complex and ever-changing world. To be able to deliberately respond to our current circumstances, both inner and outer, we must constantly calibrate and align our actions with our objectives and values.

How we manage our time day by day essentially adds up to how we end up managing our life. It takes a lifetime of exploration and growth to create the life we deeply desire and it's essential that we keep adjusting based on what we discover from our experiences.

You probably picked up this book because:

- You are a driven and capable individual who sometimes feels overwhelmed by all your responsibilities and you sometimes struggle to prioritize and make decisions.

- You feel pulled into a whirlwind of demands and have lost connection with the "bigger vision" for your life. Life seems to "run you."

- You long for an approach that doesn't just help check things off your to-do list, but helps you determine what's on there in the first place.

- You have dreams and ambitions about what you really want to experience or accomplish in this life and the positive impact you want to have, but somehow those dreams keep getting relegated to the back seat. You feel it's time that your dreams are brought forward, claimed, and lived!

- You realize that, if you want to live your life to its fullest, no "one quick fix," "three simple steps," or "just do exactly what I did" plan will be sufficient or sustainable. Instead, you are willing to engage in an exploratory approach to time management in order to shape a system that will truly work for you, now and in the future.

Not Your First (Time Management) Rodeo

When I mention that I support busy professionals with time management, the reaction is almost always the same; "Who doesn't need help with that?"

I'm sure you've had those days when you have so much to do that you are barely out of bed before you are driving at full speed, diving right into all the responsibilities and tasks on your plate. It's easy to get sucked into a vortex of demands, and we plug away—one thing at a time—throughout the day. At the end of the day, the vortex "spits us out," and we land, exhausted, on the couch, wondering where the day went. Often, we're left asking ourselves, "I guess I did get some 'stuff' done, but did I really even make a dent in my hugely demanding to-do list? Did it matter?"

Getting By Is Not Enough

If you are like most people these days, you probably feel like life is rushing by and work and other demands are getting the best of you. Some of what you really care about in life gets compromised and dreams get neglected, at least "for now." Somehow there are never enough hours in the day or days in the week to catch up with the never-ending stream of demands and responsibilities that fill up your time.

You are likely driven, and have many interests and ambitions—so many, in fact, that you end up feeling scattered among them all without making significant progress on anything in particular. Your attention might be diverted to "shiny objects," and you might struggle to stay focused. You find it challenging to create a sustainable and inspired daily pace and life, one that leaves you fulfilled rather than depleted. You want to be able to look back at your life and say, "Yes! I really lived my life!"

Business professionals and entrepreneurs come to me because they've tried every trick in the book and still find it hard to manage their time in a way that gives them traction on those most important initiatives while maintaining sanity. No matter how they try to stretch and squeeze their time, it snaps back to twenty-four hours a day! Each of the time management tactics, tips, tricks, tools, and techniques they've tried helped tangentially. They got a bit more done and felt an increased sense of productivity, but keep ending up on square one, feeling stretched too thin and never doing quite enough. Their daily busy lives don't provide the true sense of fulfillment that they long for.

The problem is that most time management approaches:

- Focus on tactics
- Are too generic

There is a good reason so many tools, apps, and books are out there with time management and productivity techniques. There are infinite ways to approach time and task management. Rather than adopting yet another tip or trick, what we need to do is approach time management as an individual journey of discovery and implementation.

There absolutely is value in existing traditional time management and productivity books. I will point to some core messages that I find most useful, but mostly I want to add to what has already been written. When we know what we want—what matters to us—all those tactics can be very useful in helping us be productive and organized, and ultimately make meaningful progress in our work and our life ambitions.

The problem occurs when we adopt time management tips and techniques without also doing the deeper and very personal work to clarify what truly matters to us. When we go straight to tools and techniques, we may end up efficiently accomplishing more, but that doesn't mean we're accomplishing the things that matter most. In many cases, much of the really important stuff gets sidelined, pushed out to "sometime later."

For instance, we might implement techniques for how to manage our email inbox without considering how we want email to actually support us in achieving our goals. As business owners, we may implement a social media action plan without first getting clear about who we want to reach and what we want to accomplish with our increased visibility. When we lack a clear connection between what we give our time to and what truly fulfills us, we tend to get lost again and again. We make progress, but get little satisfaction from what we accomplish.

Many time management tips suggest that we shove more and more into those twenty-four hours we all have to work with, and thereby become more effective and achieve more. After implementing some tips and techniques our busyness might become a bit more organized, but we still feel crazy-busy. We keep trying to "carve out" time to do what feels most important.

Being so focused on squeezing in more is not only wrong, it is likely to leave us off track when it comes to the goal of creating a truly meaningful existence. It's like climbing that metaphorical ladder up the wrong wall. We absolutely need to take action, but not without first clarifying what is actually important to us personally. Without that clarity, we end up more *efficiently completing random stuff*. Or, perhaps worse, we feel our time and energy slip away into delivering on external demands that don't really matter to us. As a result, we don't get the satisfaction that we hoped for from undertaking these traditional "time management" tips and techniques.

You Deserve a Custom System

When we blindly adopt time management techniques that are "plug-and-play," they are unlikely to quite fit us. We end up giving them a go, but then when they don't fit just right, we move on in search of the next tip or technique that promises to help us feel more in charge of our time. We are back at square one, in search of the next magic tip or technique, hoping that this next one will be "the one."

Although we can take inspiration from what has worked for others, we need to experiment our way to figuring out what works for us.

This does mean that some personal inquiry and curiosity is required, because, who am I to tell you that you need to schedule your tasks and structure your day in a certain way? Only you can know what works for you. Who am I to tell you how to prioritize your tasks? Only you can determine what truly matters to you and how best to make time for that.

Each of our situations is unique. Each of our backgrounds and personalities is unique. Each of our motivations and preferences are unique. Each time period in our lives presents both new challenges and new opportunities.

I invite you to take a more deliberate approach, escape the hamster wheel, invest a little time and energy into clarifying your intentions. Then start implementing ways that will support you daily in putting your time and energy into what supports those intentions. When we have a foundation and a structure that supports us, we can manage through it all!

By working through the inquiries and exercises in this book, you get to shape a time management approach that is as unique as you are. I offer guiding principles and proven practices that you can use to organize your time and tasks in a way that works for you.

If you commit to putting in the work to reflect—really get to know your inner drivers—and start taking action based on those discoveries, you will come away with a "map" of what matters most to you and tools to continue to refine and follow that map over time. I will offer practices and principles that you can adapt to truly support you and your goals, now and in the future.

Agile Time Management

The time management approach presented in this book is rooted in agile principles and practices. That is to say, an approach that is iterative; you'll try on a practice, reflect on your experience, and decide how you might want to adjust your next step in a way that works for you. It's a repetitive process where you let each iteration inform how you move forward.

The approach is empirical, which is just a fancy word for saying that the way you will learn is through experimentation. Speaking of which, from this point onward, I promise not to use a bunch of technical or fancy terms. They tend to just get in the way of really connecting with what most matters. I'd much rather connect more directly with you.

I also want to offer a different perspective on time—that time can actually be our friend. Time is there for us as our most precious resource.

THIS is actually the essence of the book: don't try to get better at time management; rather, aim to create a rich and deeply meaningful experience of time. Empower yourself to use your time as your most precious resource. The more we make deliberate choices about how we spend our time, the more we create an increased sense of fulfillment. As a result, we feel empowered and in charge of our life.

Know What You Want

I was working with one of my coaching clients, Tina, who felt overwhelmed by all the demands in her life. She kept hashing out the ways she felt pushed and pulled in all directions by what was required of her—big deadlines at work, a boss that kept demanding more and more, kids needing help with homework. And to top it off, it was tax season.

After letting her vent for a couple of minutes, and seeing the tide of her frustration starting to ebb, I rather abruptly asked her, "Tina, what do you want?" Although we had an agreement that I could interrupt her for the sake of her "bigger agenda," my question startled her. It snapped her out of the mode of going on and on about what was not right—all the frustrations, all the by-the-ways, all the on-top-of-thats, and the piling up of demands. In the vacuum of that moment when she stopped, she moved her attention from being the victim of circumstances into a place within her where she could inquire. Tina had to stop her habitual thought train that rattled on about her overwhelming circumstances and instead ask herself that question: "What do I want?" She was surprised to realize that, beyond simply wanting the craziness to stop, she didn't really know what she wanted.

Keeping up with the "crazy busy" of her days had taken all of her attention and energy. It had kept her so busy that she realized she was not heading anywhere in particular. She felt pulled and pushed, like a little dinghy out on the rough seas, without a keel to steady her. She is not alone. Many people end up feeling swept up by demands on their time.

For many of us, it's easy to articulate what we don't want, but we have less clarity around what we actually do want. That can be a scary place to be, and we'd rather stay busy in order to avoid the discomfort of not knowing. When we don't know what we want we tend to feel lost, and thereby disempowered. I could have assumed Tina wanted more time for herself, or fewer responsibilities at work, or perhaps better boundaries with her boss or more help from her husband, but those specifics would have been premature to explore. After some elaboration and inquiry, she was able to clarify that what she really longed for was more fun and relaxed time with her kids. She felt like her work and other responsibilities always got the best of her energy and she had little capacity left at the end of a day or week to engage in play or really meet her kids where they were. This one very important priority in her life had somehow, somewhere along the way, gotten demoted to the backseat.

To discover what truly makes us feel deeply fulfilled and come fully alive requires a willingness on our part to get out of the intensely busy action mode and make a distinction between what we think we should be doing vs. what we want.

It's easy to feel swept away by all the "shoulds" and by the assumptions and externally imposed success criteria. It's easy to assume that everyone else is "on top of it" and be critical toward ourselves for not having-it-all-together. In the coming chapters, I invite you to courageously inquire within to discover more about what you deeply desire, to define your very own success criteria, and then to start to make choices that honor those discoveries rather than do what you assume is expected of you.

In Part 1 - Foundation, we will explore important mindsets to set you up for success.

In Part 2 - Inspired Intentions, we will explore a formula that will take you to the core of what matters and find your personal compass for where you want to go.

In Part 3 - Mind the Gap, we will allow those inspired intentions to guide you in selecting initiatives to more fully live that intention.

In Part 4 - Aligned Action, we will create an action plan that is deeply rooted in your intentions. You will also learn a quick way to get out of overwhelm and into focused action.

In Part 5 - Ever-Evolving Experimentation, we will discover repeatable and empowering habits that will keep the approach fresh and continue to inspire you as you create a customized time management approach that truly fits you.

In Part 6 - Putting it All Together, we will—yes, you guessed it!— put it all back together into a cohesive end-to-end process that you can continue to leverage week after week, year after year. We will also apply the concepts of this book to some common dilemmas.

A Different Approach

OK, are you ready to dive in and learn a flexible framework that you can adjust to what truly fits you? You are about to get the building blocks that you can use to build your very own time management strategy and connect your everyday decisions with your bigger life goals. Your implementation is sure to provide quick wins of "low hanging fruit," but also set you up for the "long game" of reaching those bigger goals in life.

This book teaches you how to put in place practices that help deepen your awareness of what works for you and to adjust your way of living so that your days can be more aligned with your life goals and dreams, and with your values and preferences. The formula is simple but the richness will be found in the deep work you do as you reflect and gain clarity over time. I will point you to resources that will help you create a personalized time management system supported by your values and pointed toward your ambitions. Get ready to dig in and explore.

This is a journey that takes a lifetime and (at the risk of sounding cheesy) today is the first day of the rest of your life! I hope you take every opportunity to know yourself on a deeper level and empower yourself step by step as you adjust your days to better align with what deeply and truly matters to you. In doing so, I believe you will not only find more fulfillment in your life, but you will contribute to a more peaceful and better world.

This is the kind of journey where I hope you never feel like you've reached your destination, but that you keep growing and discovering until your very last breath.

PART 1

FOUNDATION

"To be truly free, it takes more determination, courage, introspection, and restraint than to be in shackles."

– Pietro Belluschi

Time Is All We Have

We all get an equal share of time on a day-to-day basis—24 hours or 1440 minutes. Minutes and hours—clock-time—will pass no matter how we show up in each moment.

Many weekly planners and New Year's resolutions ago, I read a book called *Ten Thoughts About Time,* by Bodil Jönsson. The first thought that Jönsson offers is that "Time is *all* we have." She argues that time is the core capital needed to acquire anything else in life: possessions, health, relationships. When we give our time to another person, we can build a relationship. When we commit time to exercise or other self-care activities, we can become and remain healthy. When we invest our time in paid work, we can acquire further possessions.

When we can accept that the way we interact with a specific moment in time directly affects the future we create, we more clearly see that each choice matters. From the smallest decisions to the really big life decisions, our life provides us with a gazillion choice points, all of which add up to create our way of living. All those small actions and deliberate choices combined create our life.

Rather than being in constant tension with time, always maxing out on just how much we can accomplish (as most time management systems encourage us to do), let's make time our ally and treat it as the precious resource it is.

Mindset Is Key

Since I am a time management coach, people are often surprised to hear me say that I don't believe we can manage time. Rather, we can only manage our *experience* of time.

This idea is a huge mindset shift for most people—especially if we've been immersed in the world of one-size-fits-all traditional time management strategies that focus mostly on getting things done, becoming more efficient, and increasing our productivity. So before we dive into the meat of this alternate approach, let's explore what it means to take on a mindset where we let go of trying to manage time.

In order to get a sense of being in charge of time, we actually need to put our focus on what we can manage, ways we can guide our perception of time, and how we can enrich our experience of time. We need to acknowledge that our very personal approach to time management needs to be informed by answers that lie deeper within us. There is no one-size-fits-all.

Right now you have made a decision, however temporarily, however unconsciously, to give me your **attention** and read these words. You are probably reading this because you **expect** that something interesting or useful will be provided (I hope to prove you right!). You might even feel **energized** by the anticipation and the promise that there "is another way" to time management.

We need to let go of the elusiveness of trying to manage our time and instead focus on what we *can* manage. Namely how we can:

- Direct our attention
- Shape our expectations
- Become clear about what energizes us versus what depletes our energy

These concepts will be used to start building our personalized time management systems, and will be woven into the fabric of the coming sections.

Complex Beings in a Complex World

It's easy to learn tips and tricks, but the work lies in implementing them in our lives.

We know we need to prioritize, so why don't we? We know we need to focus, so why do we allow ourselves to be distracted? We know we need to take care of our health, so why don't we prioritize our self-care? Because we humans are complex beings, each with our own varied story and intricate history.

Acknowledging just how complex we are is a good start. We can give ourselves a break and have some self-compassion. Our past experiences obviously color how we look at what we are dealing with right now. If we want to get a better grip on where our time goes, a lot of the work lies in becoming more self-aware. With that awareness we can make more informed and deliberate choices that align with what we actually want versus being tethered to our "stuff"—our past experiences and beliefs that get in our way.

Most of us are also limited by our view of ourselves and our capabilities. Our way of showing up in life is colored by both our conscious and subconscious mind when it comes to our worldview, our beliefs, and our thoughts.

We might be very conscious about some things that influence our decision-making, but we also have a whole subconscious world that largely drives our behavior. Throughout history, medical professionals and philosophers alike have been fascinated by our subconscious mind and ways of tapping into it. The jury is still out about just how much of our consciousness is hidden below the surface of the metaphorical iceberg but it is likely much larger than the part above water—the part of our being that we are actually aware of. Although this discovery process is a lifelong journey and might be served by multiple modalities of self-awareness, I will provide some entryways in this approach.

When we mindlessly scroll social media, we might actually be longing for connection but have not consciously acknowledged that. When we are too quick to dismiss an idea, we might be doing so because we had a tangentially similar experience in the past that did not go over well. We dismiss the idea in order to avoid that same pain one more time.

Our reaction often flies under the radar of our conscious mind and we reflectively act based on our beliefs and prior experiences. When we instead take on the practice of regular and deliberate reflection and a good dose of curiosity about what is driving our decisions, we can gradually bring those hidden drivers to light and make more empowered choices about how we show up. We are each responsible for how we show up in life, and we need to take ownership of our process as well as enlist the appropriate support.

And, as if our own complexity was not enough, we live in a complex world! Our very unique complicated being comes up against other humans' complicated existence. No wonder it is a bit of a challenge to navigate!

I hope you invite lots of compassion, patience, and curiosity as you engage with the complexity of life.

No Regrets

Bronnie Ware is a palliative care nurse who collected stories that culminated in the book *The Top Five Regrets of the Dying*. The very top regret was "I wish I'd had the courage to live a life true to myself, not the life others expected of me."

Many of us have lived years or even decades according to some external "supposed to" rules. It takes both courage and curiosity to start untangling our beliefs. It's important to distinguish the awards we get when we do "good" according to external expectations versus what we truly want for ourselves.

We can choose to continue to squeeze in more of the same, more of what doesn't quite give us a deeper sense of fulfillment or happiness. We can keep "managing" all our to-dos without pausing to question the bigger "WHY." But we risk arriving at the final part of our lives wondering how it passed by so very quickly, perhaps with a sense of having missed the mark when it comes to truly living *our* life, and likely neglecting some truly important aspects.

Time *is* life. Moments, minutes, days, and weeks add up to what becomes our life experience. I hope to inspire you to set yourself up to live a life that's true to yourself, without further regrets.

Create a Rich Experience of Time

The goal then, in terms of building your foundation toward this philosophy of time management, is to be inquisitive and find ways to craft a rich experience of time in your daily life.

I've noticed that, for me, those days that feel really rich have certain characteristics. I probably do something new—explore a new place, go somewhere new, do something for the first time, or otherwise take in a new perspective. I do very different things all within one day—shifting between the activities, environments, and people I'm with. I might create something or intentionally stop to be fully present with an experience.

One such time was when my family and I were going back to Sweden to celebrate Christmas. Our trip had barely started, and as we arrived at San Francisco International Airport, we found out that our flights were canceled. We were told we could be on a flight the next day so—no biggie—we loaded our luggage back into the car and drove back home. With our bags already packed and nothing that we really needed to do, that day felt really long, in a boring I-just-want-it-to-be-over kind of way. It was a day in waiting mode, of impatience, just wanting to finally be on our way to Sweden where we all so longed to be for the holidays.

The next day we made it onto the flight to travel, via Amsterdam, to Gothenburg, Sweden. We would make it in time for the Christmas Eve celebrations—yay!

On December 23, after a ten-hour flight, we arrived at Schiphol Airport only to find that the flight from there to Sweden had been canceled. Oh, no! The lady at the transfer desk informed us that she could indeed get us on another flight, but not until two days later! That meant we would completely miss the festivities in Sweden—December 24 being the most important day of celebration there. At this point, due to the earlier delay from SFO, it felt like we had already traveled for days. Not only was I looking forward to celebrating Christmas with my family, but my kids, who were seven and nine years old at the time, were bursting with excitement to see their grandparents and enjoy the traditions.

As I spoke to the woman at the transfer desk, I could no longer hold it together. As I quietly wept, she kept typing away on the computer even more frantically, with an occasional "Let me check something" and "Hold on, I might be able to work something out." I think my tears helped, because she managed to get us on a very early morning flight the next day.

When we finally landed at the Landvetter Airport at eight in the morning on Christmas Eve, we were tired and excited. My mom picked us up and, once at her house, we dove right into doing all the Christmas preparations—what we would normally have done over several days.

My mom's kitchen table was set with a red tablecloth and the Advent candlestick holders lit up the windows. We ate the traditional Christmas rice porridge, generously sprinkled with sugar and dusted with cinnamon. The smell alone was heavenly and took us straight into the Christmas spirit. Next, we geared up in wool hats and sturdy boots, and, equipped with a saw and axe, we headed into the woods to cut our Christmas tree. Once back at the house, we played traditional Swedish Christmas songs as we set up the tree and hung its decorations, each one jogging a childhood memory. We had some quiet time and wrote rhymes to go with each present, giving away just enough clues to let the recipient have a chance at guessing the content without revealing what was inside. We jointly built a gingerbread house and decorated it with colorful candies, gave it a snow-covered yard from wads of cotton, and strategically placed little Santa figures in the snow around the house.

At 3:00 p.m., we did what most Swedes do: sat down in front of the TV with warm spiced wine (glögg), gingerbread cookies, and sweets, and watched the must-see *Donald Duck's Christmas*. That was a key tradition for me growing up and I have now passed that on to my children. Even though most of the cartoons are exactly the same year after year, and my siblings and I know most of the words by heart, this was when Christmas really started. We were no longer in preparation mode. After an hour with our Disney friends, we started our gift exchange. One by one, we listened as each person read the rhyme attached to the gift they were receiving. They tried to guess what it might be and everyone watched for their reaction as they opened the package. We ended up exchanging presents for several hours. After that, it was time for dinner, a Christmas smörgasbord. It was loaded with traditional foods like red beet salad, mustard-roasted Christmas ham, spare ribs, meatballs, and a variety of herring and cheeses—an abundance of deliciousness!

On that day many years ago, it was around eleven at night when I turned up the bedsheets to put our kids to bed. Noticing the freshly made beds, I realized that we had not slept since we arrived. It was still the same day as when we arrived and that felt completely surreal. Even though we had only been there for a number of hours, the experiences we had in that one day felt as rich as if we had already spent several days together.

I was recently delighted to discover that there is a scientific explanation for the richness of experience that I felt that day. According to Andrew D. Huberman, associate professor of neurobiology at Stanford University, the way our memory works is that each time we consider an activity or phase to be over and another one starting, we actually create a *segment of time in our memory*. Furthermore, each delight and enjoyment causes a dopamine release, which also results in a separate time segment in our memory.

When I consider that, and reflect back on that Christmas story, I can see how that day of waiting in Novato, when our bags were already packed, felt like one long wait that was not very memorable. It was stored in my memory as one long segment of time where we were just waiting until we could finally be on our way. That first day in Sweden, on the other hand, felt rich because of the multitude of different activities that registered as separate time segments in my brain. We arrived at the airport, we had our special meal, we went out to get our Christmas tree, we cozied up and wrote rhymes, sentimentally watched that TV program, opened presents, and indulged in the traditional main meal. I also experienced delight over and over: the whole family involved in decorating the tree with Swedish Christmas music playing in the background, the smells, the coziness, and the togetherness we had that day.

Being fully present as we reconnected with each other and re-experienced our precious traditions had given us plenty of dopamine hits.

I bet you've also had such days when you, at the end of the day, feel amazed that it is still the same day as when you woke up that morning. The reason I am bringing this to your attention is to highlight that we have many choices for how we enrich our time, as long as we are aware and consciously make those choices.

Turn *Off* Autopilot

At the other end of the spectrum, some days feel like Groundhog Day—when we arrive at the end of the day and our day felt just like any other day. Nothing stands out and we find it hard to pinpoint anything of significance.

When we are on autopilot, it is impossible to experience time as rich because we are not even fully present. Our thoughts are elsewhere, our attention on either the past or the future. First, we need to be able to recognize when autopilot mode is on. Have you ever driven yourself to work and found yourself arriving but not remembering anything about how you actually got there? I have. The time was gone as if I had temporarily been absorbed into an alternate universe. It was almost as if I had teleported there.

Once we catch ourselves in autopilot mode, we can consciously turn it off by refocusing our awareness on the present moment. We can add variety by doing things a little differently—to mix things up or to do things in a way that piques our interest. These can be alternative and interesting ways of doing the "normal" stuff. If we always park in the same spot, we could instead park somewhere else, even reverse into the spot rather than drive. If we always get up in the morning and go straight for the coffee machine, we could switch it up and take a short walk with the dog first. Each of these seemingly unimportant changes help remind us that we have this type of choice multiple times during the day. How can we add a "new spice" to the everyday omelet?

Consider: When you go on auto-pilot, what can you do to get off auto-pilot and make a deliberate choice regarding your experience of time, for the sake of living a rich daily life?

This type of awareness is the key to living your life fully present and with choice. This is not a mindset shift that happens overnight. It takes practice. Throughout the coming chapters, we will explore a framework for how to experience more of this richness in our lives.

Subjectively Rich Time

Although still in its infancy stage, research exists about how we *subjectively experience time* and the effect of dopamine on that experience. According to research by the Kavli Institute for Systems Neuroscience (2018), we seem to have an inner neural clock—a brain network that provides timestamps in our memory. Researchers are discovering how subjective time seems to be derived from the ongoing flow of experience. The idea is that how we experience time is event-dependent, and we may sometimes perceive time as faster or slower than clock time.

We can leverage that knowledge as we align our actions with our intentions. One way to make our time feel rich is to more often, and more fully, arrive in the now. And, once we are "there," connect to our senses to truly experience the present moment.

One time I went for a walk with my kids. We went into a magical forest that is near my house. I find it magical because of the way the light streams down through the tall treetops onto the impossibly bright green moss on the trunks of the trees and the trickling of the creek that gently jumps and skips over rocks and branches. I had brought a little picnic for us and as we sat down to have our snack we realized just how quiet it was around us. In the moment I thought of a game to play: What if we stayed quiet for a couple of minutes and really listened to the sounds of the forest? How many different sounds would we hear? At first, it seemed just quiet, then I heard the wind gently rustle in the treetops, the water softly trickle in the nearby creek, an airplane in the distance, and a fly buzzing by my ear. Eventually, I became aware of the sound of my breath and even seemed to hear my own heartbeat. That was many years ago, but I still remember those few minutes as extremely rich and enjoyable.

Perhaps you, like I, enjoy a good glass of wine. My husband might ask, "What did you think of the wine?" and I might realize that I have finished it without paying much attention. I may have to admit that I didn't really taste it. When I am absentminded and not present to the sensations of my body—be it taste, smell, or touch, or what I hear or see—I clearly miss out on the richness of the experience.

The extent to which we can be present in our day-by-day, aware in our moment-by-moment, significantly influences how we experience time and, ultimately, our life. When we slow down enough to listen to our inner voice and become aware of how we receive the world, we can make more informed choices.

Of course, the concept of time is complex and there are no easy answers. We can accept the challenge to set clear intentions and regularly reflect for self-awareness. That's how we can empower ourselves and make deliberate choices about how we use our time. If many of the items on our to-do list get checked off but we still don't feel very satisfied, we can let it be a sign that we need to inquire within ourselves: What would feel truly meaningful to complete? We can become more discerning about what ends up on our to-do list to start with.

When we can make deliberate choices every day that support us in living our life, ultimately, we can live a fulfilling life. We can take on experiments that support us in growing and clarifying what it means specifically to us to fully live our life. The time management approach you're about to learn creates that connection for us individually, making sure that what we value and dream of in our life is connected to what we prioritize on a daily basis.

No Time Like the Present

When we push out our dreams to "sometime later" rather than finding ways to include them, even in small ways, in our daily life, we risk never getting to them. "Tomorrow" is always a day away.

So many people I talk to are so very busy, often doing the things they feel they have to or *should* be doing, versus the things they want to be doing. They tell themselves that "*Soon* it will be better, and then I will *really* do more of the things that feel meaningful and bring me joy!" Yet, they keep having so much on their plate that they end up just getting by, doing the most urgent or the quickest tasks, or things with the most looming sense that they "should" be done. With a feeling of defeat, they push their dreams and most meaningful projects to the side "for now."

Even as we manage to get stuff crossed off our to-do lists, more demands get added. So we push through, go "heads down" and plug away. We keep thinking, "*Next* week will be better" or "Once I've completed this project, I'll finally get a break." But when that time rolls around, we are just as busy. That sane and spacious schedule seems to always lay just beyond the horizon of our calendar.

It is hard to challenge the status quo, and in many ways, we get in our own way. We avoid rocking the boat. We feel vulnerable when it comes to making requests because it may inconvenience others. It takes courage to stand our ground.

Of course, short term we can push all else aside, be that dependable superwoman, and meet all those demands. But In the long run, nobody will benefit from this high-stress, pressure-filled, and for some, frantic way of living—one in which we continue to sacrifice our ambitions, priorities, and well-being. Relationships get strained, resentment builds up, and for some, it leads to burnout and illness.

Here is a short story to illustrate. My corporate career rewarded working hard, and staying long hours at the office was a sign of being committed. I was actually very committed, and stayed at the office way longer than most of my colleagues and even longer than the air conditioning and the lights. I stayed fully consumed in my work, head down, often working through challenging analysis. Soon enough the cleaners would come around to empty the trash and the security guard greeted me by name with a raised eyebrow, seeming to say, "Should you really still be working?" For hours on end, the only time I got up from my chair was when the lights went out. Then I would stand up and wave my arms back and forth so the sensors would "see" me and turn the lights back on. Crazy as it seems now, what drove me to do this was partially that I really did enjoy my job. I took pleasure in tackling gnarly problems and coming up with ways to enhance processes. The analytical part of me was thriving. My physical body, my social life, my emotional self, my spirit . . . not so much.

When we feel resentment about what demands are filling our days and are uninspired by the impact we are having, we are probably not giving enough energy and attention to what we really care about. When we are too driven by what is *expected* of us, or even what we *think* is expected of us, it's easy to lose ourselves. When we give most of our energy to living up to those expectations instead of daring to listen within and courageously follow our heart, we are unlikely to feel like we are living our life to its fullest.

If, when daydreaming, we notice we are forcing ourselves back to "reality" with a defeated sigh and drop of our head (and heart), and acknowledge that "I guess this is just the way it is . . . ", we are probably giving up on a dream. Just as Cinderella looks out her window toward the castle where the grand ball is in full swing and tries to talk herself into just how boring such parties can be—but finally dreamily sighs that they can also be "absolutely wonderful"—we might try to talk ourselves out of our biggest and most wonderful dreams without even giving them a fair chance.

At some point, we've all had to put our dreams and ambitions to the side. It's a natural consequence of the amount of time and energy we have in a day and of having to make tough choices and priorities. It becomes a problem when we keep pushing our dreams aside and never tend to them. Whenever we feel like a victim of our circumstances, we might need to look for even the tiniest of ways that we *can* bring our dreams into our current life right now. We need to prioritize what really matters to us and create space for that by letting go of things that don't matter.

Deceivingly Simple

Many of the tips in this book are very simple, but simultaneously important and profound. Knowing the tip is the easy part. Implementing it is where the work lies. This is not about shortcuts, secrets, or quick fixes. This is about doing the work to get clarity around what most matters to you on a very personal level. It's about how to own your life and adopt a self-empowering mindset that allows you to continuously become more aware of your dreams and incrementally make them real. It's about making deliberate choices that are aligned with your deep ambition.

When we stop focusing on how to gain an hour here and there, and instead implement fundamental changes in how we assess what to prioritize and decide what comes onto our to-do list in the first place, we create momentum toward our dreams.

Rather than putting on a band-aid by applying a quick fix to a time management dilemma, it serves us to do this deeper work. Sure, we might gain some efficiencies in the short term by using time management tips and tricks, like time-blocking, buying a new planner, or getting the latest and greatest task tracking app. However, we are unlikely to have long-term success if we don't also connect with our deeper motivation and take charge of creating an approach that truly fits us. On the other hand, when we do the due diligence of personal inquiry, of clarifying what we value and find important in our lives, we can then let those insights inform how we prioritize and manage our tasks on a daily basis. Ultimately, these deeper inquiries will ensure we make progress toward our most important goals and create a life we are proud of living.

Most of us have more power and choice than we give ourselves credit for.

An Approach as Unique as You Are

Become an Explorer

Most of us have gotten our fair share of tips and tricks for how to create schedules, organize our to-do lists, and increase our productivity. There are systems galore, claiming that when you do it this way you will finally be able to manage time. But I am one of the few people talking about what it really takes to discover an approach that works for you; I believe in introspection, experimentation, and self-empowerment.

To find *your* way, an approach that truly supports you not only now but also in the future, requires an explorer mindset. The only way to discover and determine what supports you and your goals is to test out new ways and assess how they work for *you*.

Do *not* take my word for what you'll get out of this book, but be willing to give each suggestion a try and see what reveals itself for you. In order to find a time management approach that works for you, you need to get curious about what truly does support you. Your approach is as unique as you at this very moment, and in order to start discovering an approach that truly works for you, I will happily lend you my process to get started. It's a sturdy but flexible structure that can be the scaffolding for the very personal structure you get to build—the one that is perfect for you right now and that can adjust as you and your circumstances change.

As I mentioned earlier, I don't believe there is a plug-and-play approach to time management. Rather, I believe it takes ongoing self-reflection and an experimental mindset to discover an approach that truly works for you. The thought-provoking framework of principles and practices presented in the coming pages will guide you in taking charge of how you use your time by focusing on ways you can increase your self-awareness and make more empowered choices in your daily life.

As with any large initiative worth undertaking, the shaping of a personalized time management approach that truly works for us personally requires a gradual process of gaining self-awareness, putting practices in place, and continuing to assess if those practices still support us over time. In order for it to "stick," we need to be willing to experiment our way to what fits our personality, situation, and lifestyle right now.

Enjoy the Journey

When we live our daily lives on purpose, we are likely to work hard because we become deeply invested in our work. At the end of the day we may end up feeling physically or mentally exhausted, but simultaneously and on a deeper level, when we know we are doing something meaningful we can feel satisfied, at peace, and connected. We feel fulfilled because we know we have spent our time and energy on what matters to us and on what nurtures us on this deeper level.

I don't believe life is supposed to be easy but we do get to choose how we relate to whatever challenges we face.

One time when I was out on a hike with my sister, we were huffing and puffing as we climbed a steep trail. We stopped every few yards to catch our breath, both of us in disbelief about just how bad of shape we were in. We were just longing for the climb to be over so that we could leisurely stroll down on the other side of the peak. One time, after we had paused to allow our breath to catch up, we reflected on how neither of us was enjoying the climb. We had both been thinking along the lines of "Gosh, this is tough!" and "I wish I was in better shape" and "Can this be over soon, please?" Before continuing our hike we got curious as to how this mindset was actually shaping our experience and wondered, "How could we make this more enjoyable?" We realized that to make the experience different, we needed to deliberately replace our thoughts. When we started walking again we consciously chose thoughts like, "This burning in my thighs is making me stronger" and "Each huff and puff is expanding my lung capacity." Suddenly we were speeding up the hill with determination and inspiration. By replacing our thoughts alone, we had a completely different experience of the same steep climb and the same demand on our bodies. We were moving with a new sense of motivation, knowing we were *in the process* of reaching our goal of being in better shape. We took satisfaction in the hard work.

The way research and scientific knowledge explain this is related to dopamine. When we find enjoyment in doing something, dopamine is released, which increases motivation. Huberman highlights that we don't just get a dopamine "hit" from our accomplishments (in our case actually reaching that peak), but we can also trigger dopamine release by finding ways to *enjoy the pursuit*. When we find enjoyment in the doing or the seeking, that in itself triggers a release of dopamine, which in turn increases our motivation.

Although it is important to know our direction—what peak we are headed for—to access sustained motivation, it is equally important to find ways to enjoy the pursuit, or the actual work that will get us there. Let's aim to be fully present in the hard work. When we find satisfaction in the doing, we create richness in our daily lives.

When it comes to structure, the goal is to create *just enough* support without feeling overly constrained. When you commit to the continuous work to adjust to what actually best supports you right now, you can find the perfect balance of structure and spaciousness. The right amount of structure actually supports flow and gives you space for spontaneity. Structure is what provides you with the possibility of deep fulfillment as well as lots of freedom.

More Than Disciplined Action (Energies)

As you have hopefully gleaned from what I've shared so far, this book goes beyond a traditional, achievement-driven approach to time management. I would describe that traditional approach as driven by masculine energies, which is neither a positive nor negative thing, it is simply a descriptor. When I talk about *masculine* energies, please note that this is *not* to be confused with male, and *feminine* energies are not female. Wherever we identify on the male-female spectrum, or somewhere entirely outside of those definitions, we can all tap into and leverage both masculine or feminine energies as needed.

The masculine energies are often connected with being action-oriented and having discipline and structure. We tend to associate courage, power, and forcefulness as masculine qualities. A masculine approach focuses on the practical and tactical, and aims to problem-solve, accomplish goals, and win.

One of the additional energies I encourage us to invite into time management is the feminine energies. These energies are often associated with compassion, patience, and allowing things to organically take shape. It's a more introspective, fluid energy that gives space for being/reflection. The qualities of the feminine are holistic, intuitive, and unfolding. When we include these energies in time management, it can help us be more compassionate toward ourselves as we try to get a handle on it all.

It's not that the masculine qualities of traditional time management are not useful; they absolutely have their place, but I think their focus almost exclusively on action (and very little introspection) limits their impact. We are definitely served by those powerful masculine energies into doing/action that leads to progress. But as we've already discussed, if we aren't clear on our values and priorities, that forward motion can turn into a hamster wheel.

Just the act of slowing down is hard for many. In the fast-paced world we live in, it can be scary to pause for even a moment. However, in order to enter this very different, reflective mode, we need to extract ourselves from the "doing mode" long enough to access other perspectives. With that space, we can increase our self-awareness and explore a multitude of options.

When we are so very busy, it will feel completely counterintuitive to slow down. Perhaps you're thinking: "If I were to slow down, I would *fall even further behind* and *feel even more stressed.*" Determination and action definitely get us closer to our goals. The problem occurs when we are all about go-go-go, and never stop long enough to consider what we really want. It takes courage to get out of our action-oriented comfort zone and create space to discover new ways and new resources. Later on, I'll share a little bit about how neuroscience explains these different "modes" and how useful it can be to be able to consciously switch between the two.

Tap into the Child in You

The third energy I suggest we allow in our approach is that of the child. As adults, we tend to take ourselves way too seriously! It can serve us well to tap into the playfulness and willingness to explore that is inherent in children.

One child quality that will serve us well is *curiosity*. When we tap into curiosity, we are more likely to discover new approaches, even as circumstances change. Curiosity will help us find alternative ways and identify what specifically about an approach works or does not work for us. With a lack of curiosity, we are more likely to be judgmental and less open to ideas and new possibilities.

Another essential aspect of "the child" that we can tap into is *play*. Because when we do something that feels important, it is all too easy to become serious, tense, and even judgmental toward ourselves. I am a recovering "controller" myself, and used to be very judgmental. A core part of my work now is to support others in *playfully doing important work!* In later sections in the book, we will explore how these different qualities and energies can help you find a balance between the driven and goal-oriented masculine, the fluid and patient feminine, and the playful and curious child, all in service of creating a rich and fulfilling daily experience. It will not always be explicitly mentioned, but I believe these different energies will be *felt* throughout the book.

Yours to Build

Now that we've established that, rather than trying to manage time, we're going to focus on managing what can be managed, we will bring our attention and energy to creating a personalized approach to how you can experience time as rich and deeply meaningful, now, and even more fully in the future.

After reading and implementing the suggested practices provided, you will:

- Have an increased sense of awareness and start taking action that leads to a life lived on purpose and aligned with what you value

- Be equipped with reusable methods and structures to use daily, weekly, and monthly to guide you in making sure you commit to that which feels meaningful to you

- Be more aware of how you want to allocate your time to deeply fulfilling projects and create a sustainable pace

- Understand how embracing experimentation and exploration as a means to personalize these methods will help you find what truly works for you

You get to tap into the courage within you that, in turn, broadens the possibilities of how you can accomplish many deeply meaningful initiatives in this lifetime. You'll empower yourself to make choices that feel aligned with this deeper place within you.

In the coming chapters we will dive into the nuts and bolts of how you can apply the teaching to find more richness, fulfillment, and a sense of "enoughness" in your daily life. We will first uncover your most *inspired intentions,* then create a plan of *aligned action,* and last but absolutely not least, adopt an *ever-evolving* mindset that will not only help you adjust to your preferences now, but that can also grow with you.

PART 2

INSPIRED INTENTIONS

"Do what you feel in your heart to be right—for you'll be criticized anyway."

– Eleanor Roosevelt

Following Your Dream – A Radical Act

Living your life according to what is most meaningful and fulfilling to you is indeed a radical act.

We all allow ourselves to be shaped by the world around us. The expectations related to societal norms and the opinions of family, friends, and others around us influence our choices daily. Of course they do. The problem arises when we adopt others' expectations of us as a measure of success and allow them to *limit* the extent to which we live our lives. We dismiss our own wants, needs, and desires as unrealistic and perhaps even selfish dreams.

Often we are unaware (and it can be hard to admit, even to ourselves) just how many choices we make according to what we *think* is *expected* of us. Due to all our daily demands, we end up tucking away our life's dreams in the "maybe someday later" of our heart's filing cabinet. That is, if we even dare to dream. Many of us live with limiting beliefs about what is possible and we are waiting for the "perfect time" when we will finally live the life we truly desire.

May you dare to imagine, have the courage to hope, and commit to the radical act of following your dreams!

In the coming pages, we are going to talk about the steps of creating *your* most authentic life—radically reclaiming the way *you* want to live your life, step by step. You've *got this*!

Radical, How?

It is a radical act to live our lives in a way that feels truly fulfilling because it's radical in itself to assess how our life has unfolded so far—to dare to question expectations from our family, society, or culture that attempt to determine how we live. It is radical to question whether the people we surround ourselves with are the people who will actually support us as we find and claim this fully fledged version of ourselves. How can we make sure that we are deliberate about who gets to influence what it means to live *our* life to its fullest?

What if the people around us are not ready? What if they don't like where we are headed? Often, people like us to stay where we are, as we are. What are we risking by going for our dreams? This question is at the core of why it is a radical act to follow our dreams. It's important to create awareness around who's on our team, supporting us. Who is pulling us down, holding us back?

Anyone who is in our way is probably afraid of change and of what we might become. That can include ourselves. So, it's important to ask ourselves: "What am I afraid of? What might happen if I pursue my dreams? What might happen if I don't? What's to win, what's to lose?"

We know what we have, and we can imagine reasonably well how our future will unfold if we continue as is. We are often not as clear about what an alternative future would look like.

These are all questions we will explore in different ways in this book. Once we are more clear on the answers, we can deliberately choose how we approach each dilemma or perceived obstacle. Step-by-step, and through small experiments, we get to uncover what truly gets in our way.

The first step forward to (re)discover and clarify our dreams is to s-l-o-w d-o-w-n. Get off the hamster wheel and be present for a more introspective type of activity. That in itself can feel counterintuitive and pretty radical in this fast-paced world.

When we dare to dream and take time to get really clear about what we want (dare to imagine the best-case scenario—dare to hope!), we get to realize that we have a choice: we either *take steps* to follow that dream or we *don't*! Dreaming big feels vulnerable because we might then end up disappointing not just others but, more importantly, *ourselves*. We get our hopes up, and then we don't pursue and follow through on those dreams. Ouch, that's quite a punch in the gut!

Many people go through this cycle—dream, fail to achieve, take the gut punch—and over time it gets harder and harder to dare to dream, and especially to try again to achieve. Usually the reason for the failure was in the way they approached the dream and took early obstacles as a sign to give up. Rather than seeing each attempt as an experiment to learn from, they interpret each seeming "failure" as a sign to quit, as if it wasn't "meant to be."

Allowing this most authentic version of ourselves to emerge to live the fullest version of *our* life is a radical act because we have to *own up* to living our unique and most fulfilling life. That means making choices in our daily life that support our life goals and dreams (to whatever extent those are clear to us right now), whether "popular" or not, whether easy or not. It means we dare to claim our dreams and keep doing the work to achieve them, even when it is uncomfortable or makes us look clumsy, or—heaven forbid!—unprofessional.

The challenge is that we live in a constant tug-of-war between what we think is expected of us—what will ensure that we remain accepted as one in the "tribe"—and what our unique soul's longing is calling us to pursue. Without going into the details and complexity of all that "belongingness" entails (which is a complex psychological construct that is still being researched), I think we have all experienced situations where we chose to live up to what seemed to be expected of us rather than following our inner guidance. As a child, I wanted to be seen as practical and capable just like my parents were, although I was curious about spirituality and the mystical. As a teen, I did my best to dress fashionably as a way to fit in, although I felt drawn to a more bohemian style. In my corporate career, I let my brain take the lead when I really wanted to follow my heart. It's easier to go with the flow because we don't need to defend a different viewpoint, stand, or preference. We don't risk being excluded from the tribe for being different.

Considering how essential belongingness is for our well-being as humans, it's easy to see how "rocking the boat" and going against what is generally accepted in our tribe is scary. When we go after our soul's longing, even though "our people" disapprove—be it our family, our culture, the industry we are in, or the expectations of society at large—a primitive and partially subconscious fear of being rejected is likely to kick in. Later in this book, we'll explore ways to conquer that fear and do it anyway, without necessarily making drastic changes to the tribes to which we belong.

Going after our dreams is also a radical act because, quite frankly, most people don't.

How is this related to time management?

If we want to create a truly rich existence by the way we manage our days, we need to tune into our bigger goals for guidance and direction. We take action and, over time, allow our path to reveal itself through experimentation.

This time management approach will serve as your foundation and will likely shift your understanding of time and the way you relate to time. I want us all to feel that we are using our time well, that at the end of a day, a week, or a year we can say to ourselves, with conviction: "*Yes*, I lived that. I accomplished something that is meaningful to me. Giving my energy and attention to that was so worth it!" When we can bring that kind of intentionality to how we show up in our *daily* life, we actually set ourselves up for creating a life that we are fully experiencing and that gives us a deep sense of fulfillment.

Daring to Dream about Another Career (My Story)

At the tender age of twenty-four, I took a job at a software company in Gothenburg, Sweden. My plan was to work there for a year or so while I figured out what I *really* wanted to do. I was young and ambitious, innately curious, and eager to "figure things out." Surely I would soon discover my path.

Fast-forward to twenty-four years later. I found myself living on the other side of the world, married to a dutchman, a mother of two spunky, adorable little kids, and having worked half of my life at that same company. Crazier still was that I had ended up in the IT department. A career in tech? How did *that* happen!?

At some point, however, about halfway into that career, I remember starting to sense that something was missing, that this was not really my chosen path. Although I was skilled at analyzing, organizing, and implementing systems—and truthfully, I enjoyed many aspects of my work—at some deeper level, I knew this was not *the* career for me. I wanted to work with people in a way that mattered on a more personal level. I realized that some core part of me was being tucked away and largely neglected.

Through a series of explorations, I began rediscovering these left-behind parts.

At a workshop offered through my employer I completed a values exercise. Not surprisingly, I identified my top value as "spending time with family and friends." The values that were tied for second place, however, provided my wake-up call. They were: "serving others" and "helping society." The facilitator of the workshop came over to look at my self-assessment. He leaned in and uttered under his breath, as if afraid to be found out by a lip-reader, "I don't usually say this, but . . . uhm . . . you might want to look for a different career."

If I only knew what career that would be . . .

I had been with the same company for over two decades, worked in several different countries and had never become stagnant in any one role. I'd been growing all along. Yet, I became determined to *not* celebrate my twenty-fifth anniversary there.

At the time, I already had a habit of writing year-end reflections, and each year I imagined what I wanted for the new year. My reflections included inquiries about what I was most proud of and what had touched me most deeply, as well as ways I'd grown from different challenges. I then turned my gaze to the future and allowed myself to dream up ideal circumstances and situations in the years to come. Based on that, I came up with some action that I wanted to take in the new year.

One year, in January 2013, my heart sank as I looked back at my journals from the past few years and realized that the same dream kept appearing, but I had not given it much focus. My recurring dream was about shifting my career away from one that was centered around systems and processes (and the corporation's bottom line!) and toward a more human-centered and soulful profession where I got to have a more direct, positive impact on people's lives. Yet, each year I had kept moving along the same old tracks. I didn't know exactly what I wanted to move toward, so I stayed where I was. I realized that, unless I took action, I could easily end up letting another five (or twenty!) years go by and still be on this less-than-fulfilling path.

There was a lot at stake. I was asking myself: How can I leave something that is actually really good? How do I leave colleagues who had also become friends, and some who felt like family? We had been through so much together and spent intense time together up against deadlines and "go-lives." My corporate job was great in many ways, but it was not well aligned with what I most deeply valued and wanted. I had to give my dream a chance.

When we can start to pay attention to our energy levels, and our beliefs and thoughts, we can learn to tune into the frequency at which our dreams are signaled. To discover and follow our dreams does require a willingness to listen in. It does require that we avoid judging our dreams. And it does require the radical act of actually pursuing and starting to live our dream.

If we never dare to inquire within about what we want, how can we prioritize our days, our time, and our tasks in a way that feels fulfilling?

If we take an unfulfilling scenario as "just the way things are," we essentially give others the power over our life. We take the seemingly easier road, but one that is likely to lead to regrets later on.

Going outside Our Comfort Zone

Here is a profound but simple illustration, related to playing too small, that I came across a few years ago:

That simple diagram spoke to me from the very first glance—this idea that being willing to be uncomfortable was *required* in order to experience something seemingly magic. It felt so very true to me. I fully bought into the idea that in order to gain something we have to risk something, and that with any risk there is some level of discomfort. Yet, it would be worth it for the sake of gaining something extraordinary, something *magic*.

In your experience, would you say that growing included some level of discomfort?

For the really big growth moments, it was probably not a matter of only slight discomfort. You probably worked hard and might even have suffered for the sake of creating that magic in your life. When we know that our goal is really important, we are more likely to stretch ourselves and do the work required to get there. We might choose to sacrifice, for the time being, other important aspects of our life for the sake of accomplishing this one important goal. We might have pursued a degree, written a book, or moved across the country (or world!). We probably put in long hours and lots of energy to make it happen.

The boundary of our comfort zone is also elastic. As much as it can extend by being stretched outward, it will also pull back when not being stretched. If we say no to anything that feels unfamiliar, new, or otherwise outside our comfort zone, and always choose what we know will provide comfort, our options will be fewer and fewer and our world will become smaller and smaller.

The key here is that we have a choice. Because if we don't pursue something outside our comfort zone, if we are not willing to have some level of discomfort, what does that say about us? That we are lazy? Too scared? Maybe that we want to leave well enough alone? Perhaps our life feels just fine and there's no urgency to stretch.

Sure, we might occasionally choose to withdraw into our comfort zone to relax and find, well, comfort. It can be a great place to hang out to recharge. However, when we always prioritize familiarity and convenience over growth and progress toward our goals, our world will start to stagnate.

Staying in my corporate career would undoubtedly have provided me with a comfortable life. I know it seemed like the most reasonable and responsible choice to most people around me. To me, however, it was a way of settling for "good enough I guess." It would have meant giving up on what I was really longing for. Fortunately, I realized that if I continued on my (then) trajectory, I would end up regretting not truly living *my* life. I felt a longing at my core, a tugging of my soul, calling me to pursue something of deep meaning and enjoyment. As I dared to listen to this part of myself, the pull gained strength. A lot was at stake either way. If I stayed, I would never know if a different path would be more fulfilling. Imagining feeling regret at the end of my life made my heart sink. If I did take the leap, I might fumble, fall flat, and come crawling back, tail between my legs, begging to have my old "golden" life back. My dream would be crushed and I'd have to reluctantly settle back into those same gilded handcuffs. I was afraid of failing.

A lot was at stake, but I decided I was willing to stretch beyond my comfort zone for the sake of truly living *my* life. With the support of a coach, I stepped up to the edge of that cliff, getting ready to jump.

When we choose comfort, we tend to repeat what we've already done, stay with what we already know, and be pretty sure that we can successfully complete it. We might take minimal steps toward growth, but we are afraid to go all-out, risk looking stupid, lose face. . . . We need to be willing to go for our dreams, follow our inner compass, and chase meaning even when it is uncomfortable, even when it feels awkward, and even when we feel temporarily incapable or embarrassed.

It's a balancing act between risk and potential. It can be the responsible choice to take small incremental steps and be patient, but when we get too protective of our comfort zone, we can inadvertently also get in our own way of living our life fully. The overly protective boundary can make us fearful. One way to loosen this grip is to ask ourselves, "What am I actually protecting myself from?" How *can* we direct our attention toward what we can do to feel safe enough to step into unknown territory? What boundary can we set that allows us to step out and risk discomfort, yet is worth it because that's the path we need to walk in order to reach our life's ambition? Rather than closing the door on our dream, we can identify smaller steps we can take to get ourselves ready to step out into the "big world."

When we take this approach of inquiry into what risks and rewards might result and take deliberate steps to expand our comfort zone—in small steps or big leaps—our chances of tapping into that magic come within reach, and we can make our dreams come true.

Playfully Doing Important Work

The more clear we become about what dream(s) we want to pursue, what our core values are, and what is most meaningful to us, the more fluently we can make choices in our daily lives.

You might not think of yourself as someone on a grandiose search for your "life's purpose," but most of us feel there is something in us that is meant to be fulfilled. We sense some "pull" toward an impact that we would like to have on this world, perhaps a subtle inkling that there is something we want to discover or create.

Maybe you dream of more time for a passion project and that inner dream-slayer says, "I have way too many responsibilities as it is. There is just no way I can make time for it."

Maybe you dream of leaving an uninspired career for more creative and meaningful work, but an inner doubt says, "Who am I kidding? It's too late! I'm too old for a change like that."

Maybe you long to go away for a delicious retreat away from it all, but your dream is immediately crushed by a reminder that "I have neither money nor time for that."

Maybe you want to pursue the dream of writing that book, but are met with a doubtful internal voice saying, "I'm not *really* a writer, and anyway, who would want to read what I have to say?" (I sure know that one, yet, here you are holding this book in your hands!)

Our ambitions are unique and nobody's dreams are "better" than anyone else's. I believe that *every person* who lives their life offering what they are uniquely meant to contribute not only comes fully alive, but *makes the world better off* for it.

Perhaps we want to have an impact in our most immediate world: our family and our friendships. Perhaps we want to improve something or support those who are suffering in our community. Perhaps our attention is more on the world at large—the environment or working

to resolve some type of national or global crisis. Our mission might be big or small, external or internal.

The gravity of the question or mission can cause us to become overly serious. This is one place where it can help to invite the energy of the child. We can add some lightness to our approach and be open to trying experiments, as if we're in a sandbox, testing our limits in order to figure out our capacity. With a playful approach, we can access more possibilities. It's possible to pursue deeply important projects with lightness, and even with a sense of adventure and playfulness. We can hold our discovery process more lightly and not expect ourselves to already know. There is no rush. Once we do gain clarity, we can move directly and deliberately toward that, but we can start before we have a full and completely clear vision.

Now, consider for yourself:

- What ideas and potential initiatives tickle my curiosity and ignite those spark plugs for me?

- What might surface if I pay attention to my dreams and I allow them to show up?

Your Emerging Life's Purpose

Most people I meet have a feeling they are *supposed* to know what their life's purpose is, and feel somewhat insufficient or lost because they don't quite know. They wish they had more clarity. They wonder: "How will I even know that I *found* my purpose"? "What does a 'meaningful life' look like to me?"

For most of us, finding our personal purpose is best approached as a lifelong discovery process. It requires reflection and soul-searching. The "seed" of our life's purpose might very well be there from the beginning, but the way our life's work and our contributions exactly become realized is something that evolves and reveals itself as we fully participate in and experience life.

Some find their life's work based on suffering—a significant loss, a tragic life event, or an experienced injustice. They might make it their mission to *not* have others suffer in the way they have. For others, it is about a specific problem to be solved, finding a cure, or perhaps inventing or creating something new. Still others might want to offer their unique abilities for the benefit of a certain group of people. And for some, their life's purpose is more subtle—more of a quality of being that they bring to the world. The list of possible purposes is as endless and unique as we each are (one in a gazillion!). I have no doubt there is a need in the world that you are uniquely qualified to meet.

Perhaps you are one of the lucky few who are crystal clear about your life's purpose. If so, congratulations! Keep reading, as the following elaboration will help you connect to it in a deeper way and help guide you in your daily decision-making.

A powerful way to answer this bigger-than-life question, and gain clarity about our life's purpose, is to look at it from multiple perspectives. If we compartmentalize in order to get clarity on the pieces, then we can put it all back together into a cohesive and integrated "picture" using discovered themes and core values. Using this process (which will be explored in detail in chapters 5 and 6), you'll create your own "map," which will help guide you in living your life with integrity and a sense of soulful satisfaction on a daily basis.

You get to clarify your deeper "drivers" by identifying what is truly important to you in different aspects of your life. That clarity, in turn, will help you make decisions about how you want to spend your time on a daily and weekly basis. Ultimately, you will align your actual life more fully with the life you deeply desire.

The First Step to Success: Define Success

If we are truly in the pursuit of a fulfilling existence versus validation from the outside that we are *considered* successful, it is essential to do the inner work of defining our own very personal definition of success.

According to the *Britannica* dictionary, there are two essential meanings for "success":

1. the fact of getting or achieving wealth, respect, or fame

Unfortunately, our society largely considers someone successful based on this definition of someone wealthy, highly respected, or famous. Unless we get that external validation of respect or fame, or the financial proof of wealth, how can we claim "success"?

2. the correct or desired result of an attempt

It is more useful, in order to set ourselves up for a successful life, to create our very own definition of what it would mean to achieve the desired *result of an attempt*. If we don't first define our "desired result" we can never be successful. If we are not first clear about what would be the "correct" result, how can we ever claim success?

As pointed out in *The 7 Habits of Successful People* by Stephen Covey, we need to *start with the end in mind*. He guides us to do so for specific initiatives and projects, and emphasizes the importance of being really clear about what we are aiming to create. But I believe we need to take a bigger view. If we were to "begin with the end in mind" for our *life,* what would our definition of "a life well lived" be? What goals would you set for yourself?

Although it is a lifelong journey to create that, I believe we are well served to imagine and start creating that life now. After all, each moment, each relationship, each activity we engage in is what will add up to our life. What we are deciding to focus on *now* is what we get to reflect back on at the final stages of our life.

When you reach the end of your life, what will stand out as meaningful memories and accomplishments? What aspects of your life will have contributed to making it truly rich? Each of us has to discover our own specific definition of what a "life well lived" means.

What we have been fed as examples of success are often the big "splashy" public accomplishments—something of significance that the world notices—perhaps a significant launch, an appearance on television, or a headline-inducing feat. Other examples are more personal, like completing a degree or getting certification, or maybe throwing a really fun fiftieth disco birthday party (yes, you bet, I had one of those!). Most people would agree all these scenarios can be described as successful.

But what about the more subtle, step-by-step successes along the way— each of the smaller achievements that lead up to breakthroughs and larger successes? To what extent are we consciously considering this progress along the way as successful?

As mentioned earlier, our dreams and desires can easily get put in the shadows of the many *supposed to's,* we are trying to live up to. Discretely, when nobody's watching, we might dare to briefly consider them, but when daily demands take our attention, we quickly stuff that longing away with a sinking feeling in our heart and an aching thought of "maybe someday." *Maybe someday, when all my current responsibilities subside and give space, then I will dare to let my dreams roam free and frolic over the pastures of paths still to be discovered.*

You may very well end up *considered* successful in an external sense, but I want for you to find ways to *feel success* on a daily basis, from the very first steps toward a larger goal. According to your very own inner definition of success—be it a sense of fulfillment, peace, meaning, connection, or accomplishment—you can incorporate action that takes you closer and closer, starting now.

Defining Success

I lost my father to this lifestyle of pushing through no matter what. My dad was a driven man. He worked hard and provided for our family. He was a strong role model and, although it was rarely explicit, he believed in a clear "right" and "wrong." He took a strong stand for what he believed in and when he committed to a goal he went all-in. Rather than buying a sailboat, he built one, spending many hours out in the sawdust of the cabinetry building. In fact, that is how I still picture my dad—in his overalls, his beard and hair full of sawdust. As far as temperament, I was always told I was the child most like my dad and I took pride in showing him that I was a tough girl, that I did all the "right" things.

Many years earlier, my mom and dad owned and ran a grocery store. One time he got sick with the flu. It was a persistent and strong virus and, as strong as he was, it knocked him down. Nevertheless, he had a business to run, so he went to work. This exertion caused an infection in his heart, which damaged one of his valves. Fortunately, he ended up living many more years.

Eventually, though, he needed surgery and tragically his body ended up rejecting the implant. When he died, he had just turned 40. Not only did he leave his young wife and three children behind, but he also left a legacy of disciplined work and toughness. In hindsight, I can see how I always wanted to please him by proving that I was capable and determined, even far into my adult life. I *am* capable and determined, but somehow this "wanting to prove"—especially now that my dad is not here to let me know if and when I have indeed "proven" myself—has often made me doubt if what I was doing was enough.

It's ironic that in wanting to prove to my dad just how capable I am, I have actually *gotten in my own way* of doing what I am capable of, and of really stretching myself way beyond my current limits. Most of us have some version of trying to "be good." We make it so important to prove how capable we are that we avoid failure at all costs. I have taken on pretty courageous projects and am always busy exploring something new, but I have been too afraid to fully claim my own definition of success. When I've considered what I love to do but it feels too scary, the "Who am I to . . . ?" voice shows up.

When our inner naysayer rears her ugly head, the better question to ask ourselves is "Who am I not to . . . ?" Dare to stand out in your full uniqueness. Stop living up to expectations and instead define your very own success criteria.

I'm now committed to daringly stepping into what I am truly capable of.

Defining Your Why

One of my favorite TED talks is "How Great Leaders Inspire Action" by Simon Sinek. In it (and in his book *Start with Why: How Great Leaders Inspire Everyone to Take Action*), he speaks about the importance of starting with *why*—how business leaders inspire when they lead from *why* (the purpose of why a business exists, its core beliefs) rather than *what* (the product) or *how* (their proprietary process or differentiating factor).

Although Sinek's examples and arguments mostly relate to business and leadership, we can absolutely apply the principle of "starting with *why*" to how we lead our lives. We can apply this on a personal level by clarifying our intentions and pinpointing our inspired *why*. Any time we get lost, we can reconnect with that *why* and let it direct where and how we invest our time and energy.

Shaking the Shackles of Should

When we pursue our *why*, it's important not to let the "shoulds" in our lives muddy the waters. In this context, shoulds are the unspoken or explicit expectations from our upbringing, our culture, and the most critical parts of ourselves. As mentioned in the "Radical Act" chapter, daring to question the shoulds in our lives might "rock the boat," and it can feel safer to stay in the relative comfort of continuing to live according to others' expectations.

What does it take to free ourselves from the "shackles of should"? We already spoke about the importance of defining your idea of success. When we align our life with our own definition of success rather than letting shoulds steer or even dictate our lives, we can start to free ourselves from the constraint of others' opinions and demands. In order to shed those should-shackles, it's essential that we get curious, do some introspection, and really start owning our life! Any time you use or hear the word "should," I suggest you ask yourself: "Says who?" When we make it a habit to check in with ourselves about how those shoulds align with what matters to us and what we want, we can make more empowered choices.

When we realize that we *created* the mold ourselves, however unconsciously, by taking on limiting beliefs based on others' opinions and from assumptions based on earlier experiences, we see that we also have the power to question those beliefs and reframe how we move forward from here.

One step at a time. I hope you celebrate every questioned should and every longing that you pursue. Because those are hard, radical acts that deserve celebration.

We are back to that most powerful question: "What do you want?" When we are clear about what deeply matters to us, we can better navigate the frustrations we face when coming up against others' agendas and priorities.

Sometimes it's a thin line between what others expect and what we deeply desire. It can be hard to distinguish what is authentically ours versus what's ingrained in our conditioning. For me, authenticity is visceral. It is a sensation that confirms that my heart, mind, and soul—really my whole being—is in alignment. When I ask my heart if it's the right choice, I get a "yes." If I ask my mind if it's the right approach, I get a "yes." If I ask my gut if I'm on the right path, I get a "yes!". It doesn't necessarily feel easy or comfortable—pursuing those really big dreams rarely does—but I feel grounded in that it is "right" for me. My whole being is saying "Yes."

When we don't get a clear "yes" but instead a sense that something is not quite right—perhaps an "off feeling" in our gut or a sense that something is missing—it's time for that magic ingredient again: curiosity. Take some time to inquire within yourself about what's not quite right, perhaps by listening to your own inner thoughts through journaling, "sitting with it" in meditation, or having a conversation with someone you know would be supportive in your exploration.

> - What are the signs from *your* body that tell you that you are on the right path?
> - What would need to change in order to make it a holistically felt "YES!"?

Dealing with Fear

It's all well and good to talk about living the life you want, but the truth is that it is a scary pursuit and fear can be a huge obstacle. So how do we combat that fear?

Live as if You're Dying

What if you knew that you only had weeks to live? How would you live? Your focus would quickly narrow to the most important aspects of your life. You would surely put your attention on what feels truly important.

In such a scenario, most of us would sort out misunderstandings and connect with those we care about. We could likely start to really live and experience each moment—to smell the roses. Our time would no longer be taken for granted. Some years ago, Mindy, a colleague of mine, found out she had a brain tumor. I remember speaking with her a couple of months after her diagnosis and was surprised by the clarity she had about her priorities and how she was living her daily life. Most of her daily busy-ness had fallen away and she could easily prioritize what was most important in her life. Fortunately, she ended up recovering and, to this day, Mindy is living a much more deliberate and uncluttered life, informed by her experience a few years back. We can all take inspiration from her experience and allow ourselves to live more fully *today*. The truth is that our remaining time can never be taken for granted.

We are reminded over and over again about the fragility of life and how quickly our situation can change. This happens when we find out that a family member had a heart attack, or we hear about a young person becoming terminally ill, or we know of a person who unexpectedly and prematurely passes away.

We have to be reminded to not take time for granted, but to use our time wisely and *really* live our lives by experiencing what is around us, feeling our feelings, and investing in what matters to us. To really live our lives. To live as if we are dying. Because the hard truth is that it's only a matter of time before we reach that final harbor.

Early on your journey, do some soul searching to determine:

- What criteria will I use to determine the "right path" for me?
- What qualities and values do I want to honor?
- What's my level of urgency in getting there?
- How can I make this journey as rewarding, fulfilling, and perhaps even enjoyable as possible?

But Also . . . Live as if You're Invincible

An equally important perspective is to live our lives as if we were twenty years old: full of ambition, with a sense that we have a lifetime ahead of us and an eagerness to get moving. Even if we are in a much later phase in life, we can tap into that energy to aim high, get into bold action, and live as if we have many decades left to pursue those deeply meaningful big dreams of ours—because hopefully, we do! We can take advice from the Chinese proverb that says "The best time to plant a tree was twenty years ago. The second best time is now."

It might sound contradictory to simultaneously live as if we are dying and as if we are invincible, but there is a lot of richness in this paradox (and in embracing paradox in general).

Embracing paradox means taking on a "Yes, and . . . " way of living. We can embrace the preciousness of today *and* invest in the bigger impact we want to have in this lifetime. We can have a demanding job *and* prioritize our health. As the owner of a startup, we can have *a lot* of work still to do to shape our business *and* already deliver incredible value and excellent services. The more perspectives and possibilities we allow, the more choices we have.

One of the most common challenges my clients are facing when they first come to me is that they never get to the bottom of their to-do list. Generally, they are too optimistic about what they can get done in a day or week, or even a month, and end up with an ever-growing to-do list that keeps spilling over and overwhelming them. It has been noted by thought leaders across the fields of science, fiction writing, and futurists that we tend to *overestimate* how much we can accomplish in the short term—weeks or months—and *underestimate* what we can accomplish in years and decades. In my experience that definitely rings true. I also know that when I *really* commit to a big goal and consistently invest both time and resources toward its accomplishment, I can achieve *a lot* in a few years. That is how I managed to transition careers and it's how I wrote this book. The key to that success is to stick with it and keep moving toward that goal, sometimes in small steps (because every step counts), sometimes on a topsy-turvy path (because growth is rarely a straight path).

If we knew we only had ten years to live, we'd surely get going *right away*.

By now, you've realized that claiming our lives can feel like a radical act. You see that it's essential that we get out of our comfort zone and question beliefs and "shoulds" in order to pursue our very own definition of success. You understand the importance of aiming big, but taking step-by-step action.

Once you've developed a strategy for facing and overcoming fear and have gained clarity about what it is you want to create or offer, that clarity will create a gravitational pull. Like a magnet, it will pull you toward achieving the goals you feel deeply committed to accomplishing. Once discovered, we can fully harness that energy. Imagining it as a force and a place you are truly meant to go, and really honoring that pull will take you places you might not have dared to dream of. We mostly need to get out of our own way, open up to possibilities, and shed the implied and imposed restrictions. What is truly in our way? Often it is our beliefs, our assumptions, and our doubts.

You've Got the Power

Yes, we need to connect to our visions and dreams, but we also need to take action in the present moment.

We need to both envision our future and live in the moment, to dream *and* take action. Yet, it is essential we recognize that right now—this week, this day, in this very moment—is the *only* time where we actively experience anything. We might purposely choose to live in the past, reminiscing about sweet memories, or choose to live in the future when we imagine its potential. But this kind of time travel does not support us when we use our time to rehash regrets, allowing them to run on repeat, or we worry about the future without centering ourselves back to what we can actually do about it right now. When we go fast all the time, routinely scramble, and rush to complete as much as possible, we live in a getting-things-done culture, chasing the potential of feeling accomplished in the future, and risk becoming disconnected from what truly sustains us.

When we can use the clarity about our biggest ambitions and incorporate that into our lives with each deliberate decision we make, we empower ourselves. Initially, it may feel like the tiny time and energy we are able to give to our dream is futile. But just like a tiny adjustment in the course of an airplane will take us to a different destination, so will each tiny action align us better and increase the chances of reaching our goal.

Action Shapes Who We Are

Just like daring to dream is a way to empower ourselves to pursue what's most meaningful, prioritizing the action required to move toward that dream is what will set us up to succeed. For each action we take that is aligned with our dreams, we further empower ourselves.

Big Dreams in Small Steps

As we allow our dreams to inform how we prioritize our time, each action we take is a way to empower ourselves. Following your dream does not necessarily mean drastic changes, like quitting your job to start a new career, or leaving employment to start a business. When we are willing to take on an explorer mindset, we discover many opportunities to fulfill our dreams. When we have clarity about what makes us come alive, what fulfills us on a soul level, we can consider ways to incorporate those values and qualities into our lives. We can then courageously experiment with these ways within our current circumstances. In my last years of my corporate career, I actively looked for opportunities for more people-oriented projects and pursuits, because that's what energized me. I got engaged in initiatives related to leadership development, agile methodologies, and employee engagement activities, all more aligned with what felt fulfilling to me.

We can align our daily living with our life's dreams. We may start with small steps, but over time those small steps can lead to further clarity, increased courage, and an increased sense of self-empowerment. With that sense of ownership of our life, we can more fully step into that bigger vision. When we start to live our lives in a truly fulfilling way, I strongly believe it benefits everyone, because the world needs more people who have truly come alive! Your gifts, your skills, your truest calling are definitely needed in this world. As author and philosopher Howard Thurman puts it, *"Ask what makes you come alive, and go do it. Because what the world needs is people who have come alive."*

In the next segment, we will take many of the philosophical concepts presented so far and use practical structures to apply them to specific areas of our lives.

Roles and Intentions as Your Guideposts

Rather than trying to answer the grand and intimidating question: "What do you want to do with your life?" it's helpful to break things into more digestible bits. You will get to put it all back together later.

We will start by considering; what are the different "roles" we are in? We will consider ways we move around and navigate our lives, interactions we have with others, and what keeps us busy.

In this context, the use of the word "role" is not in any way intended to be a mask behind which we hide, or a game of pretending to be someone we are not. Rather, it's a deeply authentic situational way in which we decide how we want to show up, for the sake of our ultimate goals in that area of our life.

Let's dive in and uncover how to use this concept to clarify what most matters to you! We are all in multiple roles in our lives and each role has a specific intention. Most of us can identify with the roles of being a neighbor, a friend, and someone's child. We might also be a parent, a spouse, and a customer at the grocery store. We might be in specific roles as part of our profession or our hobbies, or even based on our possessions. For example, I am a business owner, a coach, a Toastmasters officer, and a landlord. My role as the owner of a small business can be separated out into multiple, more granular roles, each with different areas of responsibility and different intentions. I'm a marketeer, a customer care representative, a CEO, an administrator, my own IT support, and the list goes on. Anything I don't outsource, I am "it."

Don't let this overwhelm you. In the coming section, we will clarify the extent to which you want to separate out your roles. You'll learn a process that you can reuse over and over again as you work through and clarify each area of your life and put into reality more of what deeply matters to you.

With so many demands on our time and our energy, we need accessible tools to prioritize, not only so we can make progress, but also so we can actually live our life on a daily basis. We can infuse each hour by *what* we choose to do and how we choose to show up in the world. The effort we put in to gain that clarity will be well worth it because it helps us navigate our daily life.

Ultimately, we will be able to integrate all the pieces of our life. But to get clarity about what is most important, it helps to first distinguish the pieces and the importance of each. You'll consider the smaller segments of *roles*, And, one at a time, define and discover what deeply matters to you, what you value, how you want to live. Once you have clarity across multiple roles, you're likely to find the red thread—the core driving force that is common across many areas of your life.

In order to define your roles, it's helpful to consider:

- Relationships
- Areas of Responsibility
- Self-care

Relationship Roles

Many roles describe a relation we have to another person or group of people. As we consider who we interact with, we can name those relationships. Some common examples include: mother, friend, neighbor, community member, customer at the grocery store. These roles are all defined by their relation to another person or group of people.

Take a moment and start your list:

- Who do I interact with, or have a relationship with?
- What name would I give the "role" I play in each relationship?

Now we get to the really "juicy" part—discovering and clarifying our intentions!

Eventually, we will be working to clarify the intention for all our important roles, but let's start with just one. We can then apply this same approach to more complex roles and scenarios in our life.

To start the process of gaining clarity, select **one** role that feels "central" or important in your life right now. It might be a role that currently demands a lot of your attention or energy. Don't overthink this. It is just a place to start and you will get to the other roles soon enough.

To expand your understanding of what *really* matters in each role, complete the writing exploration below. In order to not get overwhelmed, narrow your focus to just *one* role at a time. I will also include some examples from my own life to provide clarity. Keep in mind that two people in the same exact role are likely to have different intentions.

This initial writing is just your first exploration. Let it be rough and allow it to expand and flow. Over time you will fine-tune it and home in on the essence of this intention, but for now it can be messy and broad. Write out your answers without censorship or editing. It's a process that needs time to mature and "click" into place.

Please note that this activity requires some "mental space" and is best done when you feel "fresh." As David Rock states in his book, *Your Brain at Work*, "Picturing something you have not yet seen is going to take a lot of energy and effort."

For the one role you chose to start with, answer the questions below by writing for at least ten minutes about what matters most to you in this role. There are often layers of discovery available here, so keep checking in with yourself about what else is important, and then what is important about *that* thing.

As a [insert role], I want:

[What matters for you in this role?]

Why is that?

So that . . .

[Keep expanding/deepening by adding "so that..." at the end of each statement.]

And what is important about that?

[This will help you get to deeper levels of insight about what truly matters to you in this role.]

You may wish to continue exploring and expanding on what matters to you in this role. Here are some further questions that may help guide your exploration:

- What's my ultimate goal or vision for me in this role?
- What do I want for the other person in the relationship?
- When I allow myself to be in the "perfect state" for this role, what am I doing/how am I being?
- What do I value in this role?
- How do I want to show up for this relationship?

Once you feel like you have expanded enough, go back over your writing and highlight words and phrases that stand out as especially important. Whatever words capture the essence of what matters to you in this role will be very useful as you decide on what to pursue.

Use the highlighted words to formulate an intention statement—a sentence or two that captures the core of what matters to you in this role. That intention is your why for this role and will guide you as you navigate decisions and activities in your daily life. Please note that initially your intention statement might be a bit choppy. You will get to fine-tune and adjust it based on your upcoming experiments!

My answers are provided in the example below.

As a mother, I want:

My children to feel loved and valued.

Why is that?

So that *they can show up with confidence in the world and have a sense that they can truly be themselves.*

What is important about that?

I think that the more secure they are in themselves, the happier they will be and the more confident they will be that they can handle what comes their way.

(Other words that stood out in my exploration of my role as a mother, were: closeness, capability, self-confidence, and independence.)

Intention Statement:

As a mother, my intention is to support my children in becoming capable and compassionate adults who know that they are valuable. We have fun together and enjoy each other's company, and can also have deep, meaningful conversations.

The only *wrong* way of doing this is to think that there is *one right answer*. My example above might be *very* different from what you come up with even if you are also a mother. Do your best to listen deep within yourself for what truly matters to *you*.

It is important that we listen deeply and really feel into the answers. When we can connect emotionally to what we desire, we are much more likely to be motivated to take action in the direction of those dreams and intentions. This is the time to dive deep and discover those motivations.

OK, that was one role. Now pick another couple of central roles and do the same exploration. Once you have clarified the intentions of several of your key roles, you will likely find common threads across the intention statements. You might notice words show up multiple times. You might see how the ultimate outcome or impact you want in different relationships is similar. Each of those common threads point you to the essence of how you want to show up in this lifetime, what is deeply meaningful to you, and perhaps what is part of your life's purpose.

For example, although my intention as a mother and my intention as a coach are not identical, they have similarities. What I want for my children as well as my clients is that they feel grounded in themselves and empowered to pursue a life that feels deeply meaningful to them. The way I show up for both types of relationships is similar in that I want to support them in whatever way I can to create that life for themselves.

Intention in Action

It was spring and my son was about to turn 17, a junior in high school. Like most of his peers, he was busy preparing for college applications, including studying for his SAT. But most of all, he was busy hanging out with friends. He was quite the time optimist, and I felt frustrated about his tendency to procrastinate. His view was that there would always be plenty of time to prepare for the SAT—no need to study *today*. Weeks would go by and, as far as I could tell, there wasn't much studying going on.

He was scheduled to take the SAT on a Saturday at 8:00 a.m. On that Friday evening before, after a late family dinner, he withdrew to his room to chill. The evening was winding down and so were we. I was reading a book in the living room. My husband was watching an episode of a late-night show. It was almost bedtime.

I heard an unexpected rumbling from my son's room, then his door opened. He stepped into the living room, a jacket thrown over his shoulder, and raised his hand mid-step, announcing, "Heading over to Mike's house!"

I raised both my hands while saying, "Whoa, whoa, whoa, not so fast." I asked if he remembered he had an important test in the morning. Shouldn't he get to bed soon and be fresh for the test?

"Yeah, I'll be fine," he said.

I told him that, no, he could not go to his friend's house, that it was definitely not OK.

He seemed surprised by my strong pushback and he rushed back into his room and slammed the door. I heard him throw himself onto his bed and could almost hear him fuming in frustration. I saw him, in my mind, crossing his arms tight and scrunching up his face in anger.

No wonder he was surprised; my husband and I very rarely say "no" to anything. Rather than a flat-out "no," we always try to find ways to make things work. Anyhow, here we were, my son pouting in his room and me fuming in the living room. I could only imagine what thoughts were going through his head. But I kept thinking, "How very irresponsible of him to think that can head out to a friend's, and probably stay up most of the night, when he has such an important test in the morning." I felt righteous about my viewpoint, but simultaneously awkward in this unfamiliar role of "the strict parent."

I was trying my best to step into a style of parenting that I thought I was supposed to take on. It felt wrong and fortunately I paused to ask myself: "What is important about this? What matters, in the bigger picture?" I reconnected with my goal of having my kids grow up to be caring, confident, and independent beings who are able to make good decisions for themselves. It became crystal clear that me telling him "absolutely not" and me making this decision *for* him, did not support my intention. I realized I needed to rephrase the question, and to instead ask myself, "What do I want him to understand or learn from this situation?"

After a few deep breaths and recentering myself, I knocked on his door and asked if we could talk. He said yes. I assured him that he would get to decide for himself, but asked that he hear me out and that he actually give what I say some thought before making his decision. I talked, he listened, and he agreed to take a little time to think. I left his room and resumed reading my book on the living room couch. A few minutes passed, then I heard his door open. He stepped into the living room, a jacket thrown over his shoulder, raising his hand mid-step, announcing, "Heading over to Mike's house!"

I said, "OK, if that's what you think is best. I love you. Good luck tomorrow."

I'm not saying it was easy. Neither am I sharing this as parenting advice. What felt important to me was that I retain the integrity with what matters to me as his mother. Turned out, he did just fine on the test, got into college, and actually graduated just recently. I still don't know how late he stayed up that night at his friend's house. But I know that I honored what felt important to me: to empower him, or rather, to not take the power he innately had from him. That way the results were also truly his.

Keeping in mind the role for which you've just clarified your intention:

- What's a recent challenge or dilemma that you've experienced?
- How could your current clarity have informed how you approached that situation?
- How might you choose to act differently next time you face a similar challenge?

Responsibilities

Now that you have clarified some of your relationship-based roles, let's consider another set of roles: those related to **your responsibilities.** These are areas of our lives where we consider ourselves responsible for certain tasks that are not directly related to a relationship. Let's explore how you might name each of those roles and clarify your intentions. Some examples of responsibility-related roles are: homemaker, family finance manager, cook, gardener, or boat owner.

Think about your current to-do list and reflect on what responsibilities keep you busy. Jot down your roles that are related to those responsibilities. Just give each role a placeholder "title" for now. We will expand more and home in on the details later.

Consider:

- What do I consider my responsibilities to be?
- If I cluster those responsibilities together, what would I call the roles where those responsibilities belong?

You may have a looong list of roles. That's OK. Some might get combined later; some might be further separated out. You'll discover the "right" detail level as you work through the next steps. As you explore bit-by-bit, you will gradually gain clarity about your very personal definition of success for different areas of your life.

The list doesn't need to be exhaustive; just make sure you've identified your most important responsibility roles. We will then move on to the process of clarifying your intention for each of those roles.

Just like we did with the relationship roles, start with just one role and use the provided questions to unpack what matters to you. Again, make sure you give this exploration some time, at least a good 10 minutes.

For one particular area of responsibility, consider:

- What matters for me in this role? (Keep expanding with "so that...")
- What is the importance of me delivering on this responsibility?
- What is important about that?

Remember, this is just a first draft and over time you get to adjust so that it more fully reflects your intention.

Your exploration might look something like this:

As our family's "finance manager," I consider myself responsible for:

Ensuring that bills are paid on time, that our tax return is submitted on time, that we have insurance where it makes sense, and that we have a financial plan for the coming years.

And why is that important?

So that *I know that we are caught up and don't cause unnecessary financial loss or costs.*

And what is important about THAT?

So that *we don't have to worry about money on a daily basis and can be fully present in enjoying our lives.*

Some responsibilities will bring us joy, whereas some might feel tedious and/or imposing. For example, regarding my family finance manager role, I realized that what energizes me in this role has more to do with *having it be done*. Even though I don't especially enjoy doing these tasks, I know that I'd rather not procrastinate around them and thereby have them drain my energy. I know I might as well get to them as soon as possible and not waste energy by letting those tasks weigh me down unnecessarily.

Keep writing ideas and thoughts in order to deepen and expand. Explore:

- What makes this responsibility essential?
- What will I be doing when this part of my life is in the "perfect state"?

The following steps are the same as for your relationship roles.

Once you have clarity (enough for now), check back for key words and the most important aspects of your exploration. Similar to your relationship role; What words capture the essence of what matters to you in this role? For me as a family finance manager, words that stand out are: *awareness, plan, now, and in the future.*

Now it's time to shape your intention statement for this role using your key words. As an example, here is my current intention statement for my role as our family's finance manager:

As a family finance manager, my intention is to be on top of and fully aware of our financial situation so that our family is supported now and in the future.

Your Intentions Are Truly Yours

You may have a similar area of responsibility but come up with a very different intention. You might be in a similar role, yet call it something different. Your main focus as a "family finance manager" might be to track expenses so that you know your family is provided with the essentials until the next paycheck. Or, you might have the ambition to be immersed and actively manage your investments by diving deep into learning about currency exchange, real estate markets, and all forms of investments. You might even have the intention to comfortably retire at age fifty.

When we work on our intentions for a while and allow them to evolve into what feels true and deeply inspiring, these intentions will be our guide into what is the "right" next action for us to take. Do your best to listen deep within yourself for what truly matters to you both in the short term and the long term for this area of responsibility.

Example: As a Business Owner . . .

Some roles have more complexity and it is useful to first expand into multiple roles. Once you have clarified your intention for each, you might choose to then combine them into fewer sets of roles based on the similarities across the intentions. As solopreneurs, or owners of very small businesses, we are seemingly in one role—that of Business Owner—but really we are wearing many hats and each role has a somewhat different intention. When we decide on strategic goals, decide on our services, form partnerships, etc. we work *on* our business as the CEO, or one of the other chief executive roles for our company. Some of our roles are focused on working in the business when we take care of bookkeeping, deliver our services, ensure a social media presence, design our website, and *so much more*. Depending on the reason we started our business in the first place, the intentions might overlap with other areas of our lives. Our intention might include a deeply rooted desire to solve a specific problem or have a particularly positive impact on the world. For someone else, there might be an overlap in a more practical sense; they might have created the business to gain flexibility in their schedule so that *other areas* of their life can get more attention.

Here are a few examples of intentions from my clients:

- As a business owner, I want to offer my expertise and feel I have an impact while making supplemental income.
- As a business owner, I create online courses so that many can benefit from my work and I create a passive income stream.
- As a business owner, I create a highly profitable business that supports not only me and my family, but also contributes significantly to humanitarian causes.

To illustrate how the different intentions might look for each of the multiple roles we might be in as solopreneurs, here are a few examples:

- As the **administrator** in my practice, I automate and simplify as many admin tasks as possible, so that I can focus my energy and attention on delivering value (and eventually outsource these tasks).
- As the **CEO** of my small business, I make decisions about strategy and set long-term goals, so that I can focus my attention in the areas where I can have the biggest impact.
- As the **facilitator** of my Aspirational Accountability Allies groups, I plan interactive sessions that invite introspection and insight so that my participants feel empowered to have an even bigger impact through their business.

In addition to relationship roles and roles that relate to specific responsibilities, the third category of roles is that of a "human being" or of "self."

As a Human Being . . . Self-Care

The roles in this category all relate to the needs that we have as human beings. They relate to the responsibility we have to care for ourselves as physical, mental, emotional, and spiritual beings, and how we bring focus to our growth and development during this lifetime. The intentions for these roles include what brings us enjoyment, fulfillment, and joy, perhaps just for the sake of it. They point us to activities that energize us and make us come alive. As we explore these roles and intentions, we'll get clarity about how we want to shape the well-being, self-expression, self-development, and self-realization in our lives.

There are different ways we can care for ourselves but at a fundamental level, it is about making sure our physical, emotional, mental, and spiritual needs are met. At the most basic level, we need nutrition, shelter, and rest to meet our physical needs. Our emotional needs include feeling safe and having people in our lives that care about us, just as we care about them. Mentally, we need to take care of our well-being by using our intellect and stimulating our mental capacities. And spiritually, we want to feel a sense of meaning with our life and perhaps a connected presence beyond the physical world.

Again, each and every one of us needs to inquire within to discover our definition of well-being and clarify what is most important to us at this particular time.

We are all human beings with a physical body, yet our intention for our physical well-being might be light-years apart. If we were to compare two women of the same age, one woman's intention might be to be fit enough to run a marathon and another's to be fit enough to play with her grandchildren. In addition, intentions will morph over time, as we change in different stages of our lives. The intention of one woman in her thirties might be to feel strong and capable of going on physically demanding excursions. The physical well-being intention for that same woman at eighty years old might have shifted to be more about independence and continued mobility in her daily life.

I take care of myself so that . . . I feel at ease, energized, happier, relaxed, inspired, etc. Those outcomes will clearly affect other areas in my life.

When I take time to care for myself physically, emotionally, mentally, spiritually, I am so much more capable and ready to take on other challenges in my life!

Here are some examples:

- *As a physical being, I exercise and eat healthy so that I can count on my body supporting me as I show up, and pursue other meaningful goals and relationships in my life.*

- *As an emotional being, I have close relationships where I can show my most vulnerable self, **so that** I feel connected, allow my feelings, am OK with my feelings, and accept them just as I am.*

- *As a mental being, I challenge myself by reading and learning, always taking on challenges **so that** I keep expanding my mental capacity and feel eager to continue to tackle challenges and create new possibilities for myself and others.*

- *As a spiritual being, I sit in silence, I dance, I create art, I am in deep conversations about what matters in life **so that** I feel more present and connected in my daily life.*

Me, as a Human Being . . .

At a more granular level, the criteria are more specific. Physically, do we rest enough? Do we exercise our heart and our body so that it becomes (and stays) strong? Do we eat healthy food that truly nurtures our body and gives us energy? Emotionally, do we feel close to someone, do we have someone we can be completely ourselves with, where we feel "enough" the way we are, accepted, with a sense of belonging? Mentally, do we challenge ourselves in a way that we grow and expand our capabilities and make it more likely that we will stay mentally strong into old age? Spiritually, can we find a sense of belonging to something deeper or bigger and truly feel that we have a purpose in this life? People often say, "I don't have time for the gym." But if we frame it as an act of self-care that is aligned with our broader priorities and is central to achieving our goals, it will feel really different to say, "No time for that." We can start to see that we actually don't have time to *not* go to the gym because we see the connection between taking care of ourselves and our goals.

You start to see that going to the gym sets you up to succeed. You might, on the other hand, be able to identify an activity that is *not* aligned with your priorities and choose to say no to that instead.

One of my clients, Mia, was perplexed when I suggested that her work on clearing piles of papers and an overall mess in her office was an act of self-care. "No, no, no," she objected, "what I do for self-care is to take long walks, do yoga, or get a massage. Clearing this mess definitely does not feel like self-care." After a couple of days to let the idea sink in, and taking some action on those piles, she wrote to me: "Ulrika, clearing my space feels sooo good. I am starting to see what you mean, how I could think of this as self-care! I feel so good every time I am in my office now."

Let's revisit a goal that many of us have had in some variation: Get in Shape, whether that means losing weight, exercising, or eating healthier. Perhaps it entails changing some habits around alcohol, sugar, stress, or rest. For our Get in Shape example, if we were to focus on the *what* of this goal, we might end up with goals like:

- Cut down on carbs
- Exercise twice a week
- Lose ten pounds before summer

Perhaps this inspires us to hit the gym or stick to a certain diet for a few weeks. Instead, I suggest we discover an intention that can inspire us even when "the going gets tough" . . . or when we get too busy . . . or when we just don't feel like it . . . or when we feel frustrated at the lack of progress. This intention is focused on the *why*, and reminds us how this goal is worthy of our attention and energy, even when it's not easy or we don't feel like it.

In this example of the Get in Shape goal, I might ask myself; *Why* would I bother getting in shape? *Why* would I spend time and energy at the gym? *Why* would I choose oatmeal over a bagel and cream cheese for breakfast? *Why* is it important to me to weigh ten pounds less by the time summer rolls around?

Personally, my answers to those questions would lead me to realize that the true motivation behind this goal for me is to feel strong and fit. I want to be more able to live my daily life with engagement and energy, and by extension, I want to stay healthy for many years to come to enjoy my life with friends and family. I see myself actively playing with my (still to be conceived) grandkids and traveling the world with my also aging but equally healthy husband. Yeah, I want *that*!

When we discover a *why* that triggers an emotional response, it is much more likely to provide motivation to choose both healthier activities and foods. When we can identify and emotionally connect with our *why*, then we can also use it to remind ourselves when we are tempted to choose laziness over exercise. A truly inspired intention can help us resist the temptation to go for a second serving of ice cream.

What is your *why* for your well-being—be it physical, emotional, mental, or spiritual, or perhaps a combination of all? Consider:

- How does it matter to me? How will it enhance my life?
- What is the reason I'd put in the time and energy toward that goal? How so?
- What would overall success look and feel like?

Take your time. Write about it, talk about it, dream about it! Vision board about it. Make it come alive and touch you on an emotional level.

Potential Additional Role: Personal Development

Some initiatives we want to pursue might not neatly fit into one of your roles. You might have goals or interests that you want to pursue just for the sake of growth, or your overall enjoyment of life. If those pursuits don't fit under one of your already defined roles, you might want to identify one additional "role" for that. What you label this role is, of course, up to you. One person might call it "Personal Growth," another "Personal Expression," and yet another "Personal Development." Over time, with a high level of intentionality, you can hopefully embed these aspects into the other roles in your life. But to start with, it can be good to have a separate role in order to really give it the attention it deserves.

As I have discovered the overlap between the different roles and intentions in my life, I am now able to find a sense of continuous personal development within my roles. When I was in my corporate job, however, and felt like my job was not very well aligned with the ways I wanted to grow, I used to have a specific role for *Personal Development,* where my intention was to grow, learn, and expand my capabilities. I wanted to pursue activities that were creative, fun, and that helped me grow.

For example, I joined Toastmasters in order to grow my confidence as a speaker, and accepted the role as club president to expand my leadership skills. I hosted gatherings of soul-centered women to fill my desire to be in meaningful conversation and contribution to a cause that I believe in. This satisfied me on an emotional as well as spiritual level. Nowadays, each and every role I'm involved with provides many growth opportunities and I don't need this separate role any more. As an Author (!) writing this book, I'm definitely expanding my skills and helping myself grow personally, but I am also meeting my intention of sharing large concepts and the practical ways in which they can be useful to *you,* applied to *your* daily life.

The more we follow our inner guidance, actually reflect on what works and what doesn't, and continually course-correct, we get to calibrate our intentions and align our actions in a way that infuses our lives with this sense of personal growth and personal expression (or whatever you choose to call it). It requires patience and it is definitely "a process."

By incorporating that kind of richness into our intentions (and daily lives) we start to see how it all fits together and get a sense that we are fully showing up as ourselves. Once we clarify the intention for multiple roles, we might see the "red thread" of commonalities coming through in these roles. This is how our life's purpose starts to emerge.

Who Am I Serving When I'm Going on Empty?

Many of us, especially women, tend to put ourselves last. Showing up for others when we are not taking care of ourselves seems like the heroic and most generous thing to do. Perhaps it is, if we look at it from a very short perspective. But short-term thinking around self-care is risky. Just like we have a tendency to put off our dreams to "maybe someday" when we are consumed by life's demands, it's easy for us to think, "I'll take care of myself later." However, we are easily as busy the next hour, the next day, and we end up running out of energy and time to really care for ourselves. There are of course times when we have to just push through and get something done and *then* take care of ourselves. However, most people seem to keep pushing that later time further and further out. It might cause us to get frustrated, bitter, and perhaps even burned out. If we don't regularly charge our batteries, we will be "going on empty." When we are exhausted and barely hanging on, we don't tend to do our best work. We struggle to take care of those closest to us, that we deeply care about. For example, as a mom, I used to work on projects that were extremely busy—especially as we were getting close to "go live." We would pull all-nighters and go all-in until we were done. I don't think most of those long hours were very efficient, but putting in the hours was rewarded perhaps even more than the output. I truly believe that we would have produced better results, and just as quickly, if we all got a good night's sleep and then picked up the work the next day. A short walk can energize us so that we can deal with that tricky problem we are trying to solve. But feeling stuck and staying "heads down" at our desks is unlikely to provide us with new insights, and we are likely to keep struggling for much longer.

When we push our frustrations under the rug, don't deal with a lack of sleep, keep pushing through although we are going on empty, we burn out. We become less likely to accomplish what we want to and less pleasurable to hang out with. We might even lose our appetite for life. Stress management and self-care is that important.

On the other hand, when we do prioritize ourselves, set boundaries, and take our own needs seriously, we can be so much more present in our relationships, and more productive in our responsibilities.

Self-care includes speaking up about what we want and need. In order to do so, we have to understand ourselves and what we truly want and need. As with the other more externally driven roles, this requires that we stop and reflect, become aware of our wants and needs, and make deliberate choices aligned with those desires for our well-being.

Listening to ourselves and honoring what we truly want is to honor our life force. When we don't take care of ourselves, we live below our capacity, our potential. We don't have that foundation to stand on. In the end, self-care benefits not only ourselves, but the people around us, our community, and ultimately, this world. We need each other and we each need to take care of ourselves in order to bring our best selves and unique skills to this world.

When we are so busy showing up for others' needs and putting ourselves last over a long period of time, it can start to feel selfish to put ourselves first. However, the extent to which we can show up and be truly helpful to others has a lot to do with how we care for ourselves. What are ways that we re-energize, rejuvenate, and relax?

You might object, thinking, "But I like the sense of being needed. I feel fulfilled by being of service." Yes, I get that. It feels meaningful and important to be of service. At the same time, we need to find ways on a consistent basis where we can make sure we replenish the resources that we use. It is not sustainable to give and give without recharging. To "be there" for our kids, we need to feel well, have patience, be less judgmental, and be more calm and steady, which will not be the case when we feel spread too thin or extended too far.

Self-care is the *least* selfish thing we can do.

- Who in your life do you deeply care about? How well can you show up for them and support them when you are not feeling well yourself?

When we feel frustrated, disappointed, confused, or stuck (or any other negative emotion), it's helpful to ask ourselves:

- What do I need right now?

One Life

Once we have this increased clarity for multiple areas of our life, in all of our roles, we can put those pieces together and get a "map" that will guide us in creating a "successful" life for *us*.

Any common themes or recurring values can point you to your life's purpose, core values, or the "essence" of how you want to show up in this lifetime. Our life's purpose doesn't need to be grand, flashy, or even visibly obvious to the world. Small actions and daily choices about how we show up ultimately add up to the impact we have and to how we live our life. Consistently acting in alignment with our values, our most meaningful goals and dreams, can have an immense impact, even if seemingly subtle, even if indirect.

Living a life on purpose is not a "set it and forget it" feat. We need to continuously re-calibrate and refine our direction and remain responsible for our ride. We will expand on how to do that in Part 5 - Ever-Evolving Experimentation.

Having identified and clarified our *intention* for each of the "roles" in our life will help us become more aware of how we want to show up versus how we *do* show up. In the coming chapters, we will explore how to close this gap by allowing our intentions to guide us as we plan our days and weeks, and gradually make progress toward that wanted state. With more awareness around how we show up in different parts of our life, we can identify when we make more deliberate choices toward moving forward in a way that feels deeply meaningful and that is in keeping with the integrity of our soul's longing.

Once we have our most important roles defined and have connected with the inspired intentions, the next step is to mind the gap—to discover to what extent we are living our lives true to those intentions. That clarity, in turn, will inform our action-planning. When we acknowledge what fills us up and gives us meaning, it gets *easier* to make those daily choices.

Pull out *Values* from Intention Statements

Just as we might notice similarities in intent across roles (like my intention in my relation with my children and with my clients), it's useful to also look for common themes, words, and qualities across our intention statements.

A client of mine noticed that the word "fun" showed up multiple times in her intentions. Whether she considered the quality of her relations with her friends, her clients, or even her hairdresser, she desired some element of levity and fun to be a key component in how she interacted with them. Although it might initially sound frivolous to have our life's purpose be to have fun, it clearly was important to her. As a result, she became more deliberate about nurturing relationships in which she felt this lightness, and pursued activities within these relationships that provided fun. That was only one core value of hers. Other intentions informed her about her life's purpose—a key aspect being to support those in our society who are being taken advantage of.

If you notice words reoccurring in multiple intention statements or words that resonate especially strongly with you, it might be a sign you have identified a core value. Start collecting them and pay attention to the frequency with which they show up as guideposts in your life.

Here is an example of another way that core values from our intention statements can guide us. My client Tara was incredibly frustrated after each conversation with her boss. She felt that her opinions were never truly considered and her work was rarely acknowledged. Having explored multiple roles and intentions already, I asked her what the "rub" was. She reflected briefly and quickly realized that she did not feel respected. "Respect" was a non-negotiable, core value to her. With this awareness, she could go into the next conversation with her boss with a different mindset. When she started to feel the frustration come on, she straightened her back, held her head high, and reminded herself of her value of respect. Naming what was happening, even just to herself, helped her keep an emotional distance between how her boss was behaving and what his disrespect might mean about her. Later on, she would gain enough confidence in herself to have a dialogue with her boss about how she was feeling, but already in the short-term, just being more aware of what was causing the friction and changing her internal mindset significantly shifted how she felt after each of their conversations.

Our core values often point us to ways that we are unwilling to compromise. They highlight aspects that we value most in life. As in Tara's example, realizing how important respect was for her would help her overcome a challenge and empower herself to stand for that.

When we make choices that honor our values and are aligned with our intentions on a daily basis, we will gradually build a life that feels rich and meaningful. We will create a daily life that our whole being says "YES" to.

Rather than accepting your situation with a defeated "Well, that's just the way it is," I hope you define experiments to understand yourself better and, as a result, empower yourself to make deliberate choices about how you live your life.

Finding Themes

Another way to identify themes in our lives is to look across seemingly disparate roles and/or consider a longer timeframe.

Over a period of only a couple of years, I was in the roles of business analyst, expressive arts student, and yoga teacher, and was thinking to myself that I was "all over the place." As a business analyst, I collaborated closely with users in different business units to understand their needs and challenges. I worked equally close with my deeply technical colleagues to come up with system and process solutions that would meet those needs.

I enjoyed the analytical challenge of coming up with feasible solutions. In my expressive arts explorations, I discovered deep truths within myself from playfully dancing, drawing, and writing; insights that highlighted how I showed up in my life and that helped me tap into an infinite inner resourcefulness. As a yoga teacher, I connected the physical yoga practice to how we live our daily lives by exploring universal themes such as "spaciousness," "forgotten parts," and "roots" in our bodies, in the ways we show up in our lives, and in how we relate to others. Conversely, I invited my students to explore what they could learn from their physical bodies, and how we can deliberately embody more of what we want.

As I considered what was at the core of each of those roles, I realized there were common themes across these seemingly disparate interests. I realized it *excites* me to find obstacles and blocks, because of the promise of potential energy that can be freed. I connect resources with where they are needed and create flow.

As you look across your roles and intentions, you may discover similar themes that point you to the essence of your interests or your brilliance!

Stand for What You Value

I believe life can be relatively simple if we choose to focus on what we value most, although that in itself is a radical act. To dare to stand for what we value, what we deeply desire and who we are, takes courage. It's an act of self-care. Caring for myself because I think I am valuable is the best way for me to do the most good in the world. What do I need in order to function fully, to show up with the best ideas, strongest contribution, the highest level of service? What self-care do I need in order to continue to serve and show up for my most inspired intentions?

When we get more clear about our core values and let them support the way we move through our day and our lives, we are provided with that keel that can steady us as we navigate the sometimes rough waters of life. When we have this clarity, it is easier to know what to say "no" to in order to fully say "*yes*" to something truly meaningful.

Intention-Guided Life

What if you could create deep meaning and fulfillment in your daily life right now?

Life is short, and although we might project that we will live until an "average" old age, or perhaps live as long as our parents did, we just don't know for sure.

We don't have to take *drastic* action before we are ready, but if we want to truly live our lives, we must take action of some kind to increase our awareness, to clarify expectations within ourselves, and to set expectations with others. We need to work to better understand what energizes us and our vision, and what subdues our enthusiasm or kills our creativity. We need to find the courage to say "no" to that which doesn't support our chosen path, say "*yes!*" to that which will support us, and then actually take the action that points in that direction.

Coming up with inspiring and meaningful intentions and then actually *living* them is an ongoing refinement process. We might not shape a crisp intention immediately. We might not feel deeply inspired by it— yet. I encourage you to keep asking yourself what truly matters (in each of your roles) and continue to adjust the intentions so that they always inspire and feel meaningful. You can then tap into the "juice" of those intentions on a daily basis, even when you don't quite feel like it.

In addition to defining meaningful and fulfilling actions for each role that will help us get closer to fulfilling that role's intention, we continue to weave all our separate intentions back together into the unique tapestry of our life's purpose.

You have already explored the roles and intentions. Next, we will dive deep into the action-oriented aspects that are required to fully live those intentions. In the formula below, the "I will" statement reflects a commitment you make to yourself to take that action.

As a family organizer
I will plan a fun weekend
for our family
So that our bonds remain
strong and allow for
much joy & fulfillment,
now and in the future!

So far, this book has been about clarifying what matters in your life. I hope you can see how essential it is to dare to dream and empower yourself to own your path. Now, it is essential to take the next step and make these visions and intentions be very present in our daily life. Aim to make the way you live every day and every moment be infused with these insights.

Ultimately, our lives are built from millions of individual moments. I hope to inspire you to be deliberate and conscious about how you live each day, adding up to a life that you feel you have truly claimed and lived! The more immersed we are in the moment, the more fully we experience it. The more fully we experience the moments, the stronger the memories will be.

We pause in order to increase our self-awareness—our preferences, our needs and wants, our values—and then make deliberate choices going forward. It is a never-ending journey. The destination is a place we keep aiming for, but to which I hope we never fully arrive. Fully arriving would mean that our life is over, we have reached our end harbor, and we can no longer add new experiences to our memory vault.

In the next section, we will direct our attention toward the gap between what we truly and deeply desire (our intentions), and where we are currently at. We will explore initiatives that we might take on to close that gap.

When we take the time to assess the gap between what we are currently experiencing versus what we want, we can subsequently identify the action that will start to close that gap and take us closer to what we truly want.

PART 3

MIND THE GAP

"If you do not change direction, you may end up where you are heading."

– *Lao Tzu*

How to Have it All

When you add up *all* the inspired intentions for all those areas of your life, you might wonder "How will I ever make time for all of that?"

We all have the same twenty-four hours each day. Ultimately, we get to go after all our dreams, but we cannot pursue every intention with full force all the time. Rather, when we pick a couple of key projects/focus areas and truly make progress in a given month, season, or year, we get a sense of accomplishment and get to gradually create the life we truly desire.

As the months and years come and go, different seasons call for a different focus. In the spring, when it is "tax season" here in the USA, my family finance manager role gets center stage as I prioritize plowing through all the paperwork to get ready to submit our tax return. As low on the enjoyment scale as this project is for me, I prioritize it and focus in order to give it as little energy as possible. For me, the reward is to be done with it with as little dread as possible. Procrastination can be a huge energy and time thief, so I bite the bullet and *Just do it*!

Although my business keeps going all seasons, during the summertime, I take the foot off the gas pedal ever so slightly and tend to be more in maintenance mode. Instead, I expand the time I give to my personal relationships. When the fall comes around, and my business is again in full swing, I might lower my commitment to keeping my garden in tip-top shape.

At different times, different projects take center stage. While writing this book, for example, I took on fewer clients and some other projects in my business also had to take a back seat.

Other, smaller examples, would be times when I sacrificed a hike with friends to get an important work project done, said no to an interesting webinar in order to get my taxes done on time, or let the laundry pile overflow as I was committing my time to write this book.

When we can be deliberate about which important goals we are actively pursuing and consciously choose what other activities to sacrifice for now, we can still feel empowered. We deliberately put those other pursuits on the backburner, for now, but not forever.

The demands on our time and the responsibilities we have are not likely to stop, but our inspired intentions give us a clear foundation for how to respectfully set boundaries and feel grounded in our priorities and commitments.

Perspectives: Zoom Out, Zoom In

When we start from the big picture, the "zoomed out" view of our life, we can connect to our most important values and dreams. We can then "zoom in" to break down those big ideas into what will help us get traction and start delivering value incrementally. Value might be a small version of our big goal; it might be a small version of the impact that our big goal will have. Let me elaborate.

Let's say we have a *big* goal to launch our own business and make/sell our own pottery. We want to be able to spend time putting our hands into clay and creating beautiful pots that bring joy to their owners. What is a small version of this goal where we already have the impact we want to have? Do we make pots for friends, or sell some at a farmers' market? We bring the beauty into the world and start charging for it. Getting into action will either solidify our commitment and make us even more invested, or it will help us realize what is not quite on point and needs adjusting.

At one point, when I had the intention of writing this book but hadn't yet committed, I did pursue a small version of that by writing blog posts and other mini articles that I could share. That met my goal of sharing my message and my expertise with others in writing, but on a smaller scale. That has proven invaluable in shaping my ideas and getting more skilled at conveying my message.

At times, I lost sight of my bigger goal and realized that I was barely spending any time writing anymore. Still, somehow, I was thinking of myself as someone writing a book. What got me unstuck at that time was when I committed to writing at least 500 words a day for one month as part of a writing challenge. With that as my kickstart, I actually started feeling like an author. The external commitment and structure of the challenge did the trick! I was putting down my ideas and started to structure my content into what I wanted this book to be. I learned this very mind-blowing lesson: In order to be a writer, you need to write! Ha! For many large endeavors, we have to just start *somewhere*.

Another example is from a client of mine, Teresa, who wants to reach more people by speaking, perhaps one day on larger stages. To start with, she speaks to small groups at small events where people are likely to need what she has to offer. Another way she could approach that bigger vision of speaking on larger stages would be to *participate* at larger events, learn some of the "workings" and perhaps get to know some event planners. All of those are things she can start doing *now*. Getting into action in this smaller-scale way will also bring about a mini version of her desired impact that she can eventually have on a larger scale. All this doing and getting feedback will actually give her practice and open doors for her to get on those larger stages in the future.

- What's my book writing/speaking equivalent—that project I've meant to pursue but am making very little to no progress on?
- How can I actually do the work to get my project moving?
- What initial action would set that in motion?

When we make the steps small and immediately achievable, we can also better manage the fear that inevitably accompanies this stretching of our comfort zone.

Approaching the Future Step by Step

When I first realized that I wanted to change careers, I started exploring. I became really curious about what I was naturally good at, what I had a passion for, and what really made me come alive. At work, I volunteered for assignments outside of my actual job description that felt more aligned with my values. I took on an "employee engagement champion" role, I co-organized a leadership forum, and I insisted I be part of a team that was to work in a new, dynamic, and collaborative way. I looked for ways to contribute that helped my colleagues thrive.

Outside of work I explored, too. I read lots of books, attended multiple workshops, and even pursued a parallel career as a yoga teacher for a couple of years. Then, one day, while browsing a catalog to find a reason to revisit my favorite retreat center, The Esalen Institute, I found a workshop on something called "coaching." It sounded fascinating and I decided to check it out.

After the first two days in that coaching workshop, I was sold. Would you believe it? There is a *profession* that focuses on being in conversations about what deeply matters!

Finally, I had found my "sweet spot"—that intersection between my skills and my passions, with the potential of serving a need in the world. As mentioned earlier, up until that time, I had spent just over two decades in a successful career in the software industry, and for several years I'd been considering what I "really wanted to do when I grew up." I had talked myself into staying more times than I could remember. I had celebrated my twentieth anniversary a couple of years back, but now I winced at the approach of my twenty-fifth anniversary. The time had come. If not now, when?

Leaving this job, and career, did feel like a giant leap. After all, many aspects of my work, my colleagues, and the company I worked for were great. It would have been so much easier to stay and keep riding this career in which I coincidentally had ended up. However, I felt trapped in the proverbial golden handcuffs. Externally, my whole situation appeared to match the actual definition of "success" and I am sure it would feel like that to many. Giving all that up would require both courage and faith, yet I knew I had to follow my deep longing for a more fulfilling career and pursue *my* definition of success. I knew that if I was ever to make a significant change, I needed to take action before I was ready. I knew that the time would never be quite right. I knew that I could very easily talk myself into staying where I was.

At the very first session, my new coach, Laura, asked me what I wanted to accomplish in the six months of our work together. Some part of me must have known that I might get in my own way if I didn't quickly say this, so I blurted out, "I want to quit my job before the summer." I instinctively pulled my hand up to cover my mouth, as if I could catch my words and reel them back into a place of words not yet spoken. Too bad sound travels much faster than my hand, or even my instinct. I watched for her reaction, somehow expecting my surroundings, including Laura, to be as discombobulated as I felt within. My desire had been spoken. The dream-suppressing lid was off. Fortunately, I was met with an encouraging and gentle smile and a request from my coach to "tell me more." I felt the core of my being exhale and begin to relax. Nothing bad was happening as I dared to express my desire.

It turns out that this was only one of many moments to come where I had a spurt of courage followed by an attempt to recall what I just committed to. I would end up hanging out right at the edge of that metaphorical cliff for a few months.

Throughout the spring, I had many ups and downs and was trying to tell myself how *staying* at my job was actually not that bad of a choice. How I could make it work and find enough interesting things to work on? Each time, my coach asked me: Do you want me to support you in how to leave, or how to find a way to make it worth staying?

Leave. Yes, for sure, I wanted to leave.

As "life happens," we tend to get pulled into the whirlwind of demands and lose connection with our bigger vision. Some transitions take years to navigate, which is not in itself a bad thing. What's important is that we keep listening to what energizes us and what feels deeply meaningful, and let that inform our next steps.

It is essential to reflect on this gap between our dreams and our daily activities. How are they aligned? Are we actually making choices about how we spend our time that are in line with our intentions? I think of this as "top-down" planning, and we will explore specifically how to connect our high-level life ambitions with our daily action planning more thoroughly in the coming chapters.

For each of the intentions you've identified so far, assess the extent to which you are already living that intention. Rate each one on a scale from one to ten, where one equals "not at all," and ten equals "completely and fully!"

For example:

I might rate my intention as a family finance manager (to be on top of and fully aware of our financial situation) as a nine, because I think that is largely true.

Regarding my intention related to my physical well-being, (I count on my body as I pursue meaningful goals), I might rate it a six, because I realize that lately I have not been as active as I would like to be.

In my role as a friend, I might realize that, with the exception of a few very close friends, I've completely dropped the ball when it comes to staying in touch with others, so I give that a four.

Now that I see the gaps more clearly, I can let that inform what action I take, or what initiatives I take on.

Learning by Doing/Imperfect Action

When you don't know what to do or how to get started, I recommend just doing *something*. When you are feeling stuck or overwhelmed, get into action. Rather than climbing the whole mountain in one step, which we of course know is impossible, start with the first step. You might not even know which is the first "right" step, so you need to pick one and get going. There are many paths up that mountain. The only way we'll find out which is the right path for us is to get going.

If you are an accomplished rock climber, you might select the path that is essentially vertical because this is not your first mountain. You know the tools and have lots of experience. If, on the other hand, you are entering new territory where you are still exploring and learning the ropes, it probably serves you better to take an easier route, perhaps even the switchback path, and learn as you go. Both paths will get you there.

We need to choose the appropriate level of challenge and risk that works for us. We need to choose the path that matches our skill level and urgency, and that honors the qualities we want to experience on this journey. Bite-size challenges might be more appropriate for us. They add up over time, stretch us each week, and before we know it, we will have the vantage view from part way up the mountain. If we have good tools, we might work our way through jungles and dense vegetation— or we might hire a guide who has the skill and knows the terrain to help us through those trickier patches of our journey.

If we wait until we know *exactly* how we will get there, we will most likely never go. We are better off packing our gear now, preparing what we can, and going. We will learn as we go. We can hone our skills, but make sure to also apply them in real-life situations *before* we are completely ready. Yes, take small but real steps and see how it goes.

The more we are willing to be imperfect, experiment, and be open to grow, learn, and discover, the better we can be at pursuing our business, delivering value, and feeling good about our progress.

Beginner's Mind

By assuming a beginner's mind and not *expecting* ourselves to already be experts in what we are about to create, we can get out of our own way and start experimenting our way to success. We can get out there and do something, even if we are not quite ready. Such action is extremely valuable. We learn so much by doing.

Another kind of doing is to give time to reflect, get curious about what's really getting in your way (often your beliefs and your "shoulds"), and welcome (!) some mess-making. Step into that metaphorical sandbox and ask yourself, "What if…?" Don't try to prove that you've got it all together. Admit there is a lot you still don't have a clue about and be fine with that. I call this adopting a "not knowing" attitude. Being willing to not yet know means we can get curious and open to possibilities. On the contrary, if we have a knowing or been-there-done-that attitude, what are the chances we will discover something new? Near zero. Even if a new possibility would stare us straight in the face, we'd not see it because we have already decided it's a done deal.

In my business, I have not always embraced the imperfect. For a long time, I felt like I could not put anything "out there" until it was polished, professional, and essentially guaranteed to be well received. I would not share a thought, a program, or anything really until I felt I could fully defend and back up every little aspect of it. Once I started taking my own advice, when it related to my business, I felt free. When I took on the mindset of continuous learning and growth using a more experimental process, I realized that I have valuable things to offer and they don't have to be perfect, just useful. I can show my clients, my audience, my readers, that I do *not* have it all figured out. In fact, I *hope* I never will. We are all on this journey of exploration, and the process, the experiences, the connections, and the fulfillment of being engaged is what actually matters. Yes, sure, we hope to reach goals and we want to deliver quality products or do a good job. We want to honor others' time, but there's this wide "band" in the middle of "good enough" and "does the job." When you have a piece you feel could be useful to others, by all means, share it! Keep giving of what you have. Use your experience and your unique skills, and the "right" people on the receiving end will benefit. Those who need something else can go somewhere else to find it.

Grow Your Capacity Zone

Many soulful women I speak to have dreams about how they want to make an impact in this world but they are not *really* going for it. Do you, too, have a big project or dream that you'd like to go after? It's normal to have fears when we embark on an important and significant mission. How can you let that big vision inform what you do today, this week, this month? It no longer has to be a "maybe someday" project. Create a clear enough plan with where to start, and be ready to re-engage often in order to stay committed.

OK, let's assume we gather the courage to dream that big dream. We have dared to listen to our soul's longing and decide to pursue a truly inspired goal. When pushed to "go for it" and take a big leap, we might feel as if we're at the edge of a cliff, about to step into a big unknown void. We throw our palms up in a "Hold on now, wait a minute!" gesture. We realize that we are not quite ready to leap. We might even doubt ourselves and wonder, "Can I actually do this? Do I have the skill, guts, and resources to pull this off?"

In that very moment, as we're about to pursue our ambitious goal, we might actually not have the skill. We might not be quite clear about how exactly we will pull this off. We might feel apprehensive about taking the risk.

An empowering perspective is to consider how we can grow our capacity to eventually be able to accomplish this intimidating goal. How can we grow our capacity zone to overlap with our dreams and intentions? Rather than assessing "Do I have what it takes?" what if we considered

"How will I grow my skills as I go so that I can eventually achieve those goals that initially seem out of reach?" This perspective can help us shift from fear to excitement, from being scared of the big unknown of the future to a calm assurance that we can (and will!) gradually gain the capacity to achieve our big goals. It's OK to *not yet know* how we will get there.

Let's make sure you find ways to make your dream actionable and that you have a way to hold the process and feel supported. Keep steering your thinking to what you *can* do, perhaps *today* to grow your capacity—ever so slightly—and empower yourself to realize that dream eventually.

Remember that drawing showing Your Comfort Zone and the cloud with Where The Magic Happens? Well, here's a new, even more empowering visual;

Your capacity zone is already a rich place. It's where you find all the skills and knowledge you *already* have. Our current capacity zone is just that: what we are *currently* capable of. Based on all prior challenges that we have overcome, the multitude of experiences we've lived through, and the broad variety of responsibilities that we've lived up to, we have arrived at our current capacity.

We can realize that all the experiences we've had to date, and all that we are *already* capable of, is the foundation for achieving our dream. We have skills that will surely support our pursuit. We have plenty of experiences that will guide us in our decision-making. We might even be aware of some superpowers of ours that will be our "special sauce" as we pursue our next big goal!

Up until now, you have probably gained the capacity:

- To solve a type of problem
- To deal with certain challenging situations
- To produce specific outcomes
- To create/make/build valuable assets

Those skills and capacities form the foundation upon which you will make your dreams come true.

In that scary moment when I proclaimed to my coach that my goal was to quit my job and go out on my own, and the months following, how might this view have supported me?

I imagine that if I had given less attention to the scariness of the leap, and all the unknowns ahead of me, and instead focused on my capacities, I could have acknowledged what I was already really good at: I was skilled in figuring out ambiguous problems and sorting through a jumble of demands and gnarly business dilemmas. I had a passion for bringing people together and a heartfelt longing to serve. I was a rockstar at finding bottle-necks and working through them to create or restore flow. My superpower was to simultaneously hold the "big picture" and pay attention to the details.

Although I didn't yet have this perspective, can you see how *owning* these skills would have put me in a more empowered position as I pursued my new career? I believe I would have felt much more confident in the pursuit of this goal.

As I leaped into the adventure of solopreneurship as a time management coach, there was a *lot* to figure out and, fortunately, I knew a thing or two about working through ambiguous projects. It would require me to hold the big picture for my business, all the while working on the nitty-gritty of completing my foundation and getting it off the ground. No problem—done *that* before! I would have to create offerings that profoundly served my clients and all the while felt meaningful to me. What a blessing!

At that edge between my old career and my new one, this perspective would have provided comfort that I was in fact well equipped to take the leap, and learn the rest "in-flight."

Identify a small, not *too* scary, step. You know what's next: You're ready . . . you're set . . . now **DO!**

> Connect with such a dream and take some time to reflect and ask yourself:
>
> - What dream have I pushed aside as unrealistic, or even for "another lifetime"? What is my big, scary pursuit?
> - What skills and experiences do I *already* have that will support me in this pursuit?
> - What else do I need to be capable of to achieve that dream?
> - How can I grow my capacity—this week, today—to eventually achieve that goal?

Prioritize Your Pursuits

In the next section, Aligned Action, we will go into detail about how to use our intentions in our daily decision-making. In order to create the bridge between our ideal states (as captured in our intentions), and the detailed action of our days and weeks, it is useful to identify *initiatives* that will help close that gap. You may think of these as key goals, milestones, or projects. Whatever you call them, I hope you tap into your innermost dreams and desires and aim at least a little bit higher than you currently think you can reach!

You have probably heard of "SMART" goals (Specific, Measurable, Achievable, Realistic, Timebound), but this is not the time to be "smart" in that sense. Rather, I hope you reach beyond your current (perceived) limitations and capacity, and courageously aim higher than what feels achievable or realistic.

Consider what initiative, if pursued over time, would fulfill your intention in a big way. What is a truly aspirational goal for you?

A couple of years ago in a conversation with a coaching colleague, I mentioned my dream of capturing my approach to time management and sharing it as a book. I shared that not only would it feel like a significant accomplishment for me personally, but that it would feel amazing to be able to reach and serve so many more people that way. After attentively listening to my excitement, he asked: "So why don't you?" His directness surprised me and, during my temporary speechlessness, he added, "If you think it will have such a positive impact, why would you not make it a top priority?"

There I was, without any writing experience to speak of, with extremely limited knowledge of publishing, and only a glimpse of confidence that I could actually pull it off. During the past couple of years I have immersed myself in my growth toward this aspirational goal and, well, you are holding the proof in your hand. Although my aspirational goal was to publish a book, blogging was a great way to find my writing voice and start sharing value.

I invite you now to consider one of your most important roles and the intention you've identified for yourself, and think of an ambitious initiative to take on. It will probably be out of your current comfort zone. It will hopefully be outside of your current capacity zone.

Perhaps your intention as a business owner is to become a thought leader. In that case, the ambitious initiative you take on might be to become a paid speaker.

Perhaps your intention regarding physical well-being is to feel strong and energized. Your ambitious initiative might be to run a marathon or pursue something entirely different that you believe will significantly stretch *you* toward fulfilling *your* intention.

Connect with the excitement you feel as you anticipate accomplishing that big goal/initiative. If it also scares you a little bit, you are probably on the right track.

Quick Win - Aligned Action

In addition to taking on a big initiative and aiming high, you can fuel your motivation by finding a quick win—something you can do right now that takes you one small step in that direction. Look at one of your intention statements and identify *one* action that you can take today (or at least this week) that takes you ever-so-slightly toward that ideal state of your intention.

If you want to improve your physical well-being, a tiny step you could take *today* is to go for a short walk or spend ten minutes on your yoga mat.

If you want to connect with more prospects for your business, you could send one message to someone you have meant to get in touch with or reconnect with a prior client.

If you want to be more present with your kids, you could give ten minutes of your undivided attention to being with them today (perhaps right before their bedtime, or before they head out to hang with friends).

Even doing "a little something" today to honor a dream is the beginning of a radical act. This is how we build muscles. There is power, even in those first wobbly and tentative steps!

Today is when our life happens. Do one thing *today*. Do one thing *tomorrow* . . . keep going. Keep refining. Keep discovering.

Most people work on becoming more productive to get more and more done. Rather than pursuing a long-running to-do list, the bottom of which we are unlikely to ever reach, I recommend going after fewer deliberately chosen priorities and truly making progress toward those select goals. I think we are better off doing less but becoming fully invested in what we commit to for a given timeframe. Let's aim to become more productive when it comes to completing truly meaningful projects. The next section will guide you through a specific process for how to let your inspired intentions guide your daily planning and prioritization. Let's get out of *overwhelm*, and into *focused action*!

PART 4

ALIGNED ACTION

"*I am always doing that which I cannot do, in order that I may learn how to do it.*"

– Pablo Picasso

Aim Big/Act Small

Top-down Planning: From Intentions to Goals to Action!

For most of us, the demands on our time are always much bigger than the time we actually have available. We wish the twenty-four hours a day would magically turn into twenty-eight or thirty hours. We long for another chunk of hours to get some stuff done . . . or maybe to finally catch up on our sleep.

In this coming section, I hope to help you move from feeling *stretched too thin* and always playing catch-up, to a more focused, sane, and fulfilling daily life. Ideally, the process is approached "top-down," letting your intentions guide you as you prioritize the action you commit to. Alternatively, if you, at this very moment, feel too overwhelmed or scattered to even contemplate your intentions, I suggest you follow the alternate steps as shown in the section Bottoms-up Approach for Dump-Divide-Do™. That takes you through the "bottoms-up" version of this approach, and helps you free up the mental capacity required for deliberate prioritization and planning. Once you have significantly reduced your sense of feeling overwhelmed, you can come back here and go through the truly empowering "top-down" version of the approach.

You'll be using your stated intentions that you created in the previous section for a particular (important) role, and the initiative that you identified in Mind the Gap as we create a detailed action plan for how you will accomplish that.

But, you might wonder, if my intentions are so clear, why not just get into action? Most of us have multiple priorities that compete for our attention and energy. If we dive right in without any planning, we risk postponing what we really want because we immediately get too busy. Therefore, it is essential to give time to higher-level planning that will, in turn, help us be deliberate about what we commit to for a certain timeframe.

Imagine the intention trickling down to inform your initiatives, which in turn inform the tasks on which you take action.

Intentions
informs ⌐▷ Initiatives
     informs ⌐▷ Tasks
          informs ⌐▷ ACTION!

Similarly, in the other direction, the completion of action completes a task, which partially completes an initiative, which partially fulfills an intention.

Intentions ↖ fulfills
     Initiatives ↖ completes
          Tasks ↖ completes
               ACTION!

When we start putting this top-down plan together, it's useful to focus on one role at a time. That way it becomes easier to hold our overall intentions front and center and let them inform how we prioritize the tasks for that role. At a later point, we will put it all back together, so that we get a holistic view of *all* the actions we plan to take across all our intentions. But for now, we will approach them one by one. Keep in mind that you are not *committing* to anything just yet, so there is no need to worry about *how* you will fit it all in yet. Before you get into action, we will go through a prioritization process that lets the "important" to-dos percolate to the top.

Over time, using your truly inspiring intentions to guide your action and your willingness to regularly reflect for awareness will increase your clarity and focus. Your reflections will bring awareness to what you are giving your attention and energy to on a daily basis. This clarity will help you recover quickly whenever you go off track. And trust me, if you are human, you *will* go off track. The key is to catch yourself early and often, and make a deliberate choice regarding your focus and next steps. We will go deeper into how to intercept and course-correct in Part 5 - Ever-Evolving Experimentation.

It's useful to consider different time horizons—such as week, month, season, and year—as we explore potential action to take. We will explore what action we can take to bring our daily life into alignment with this intention, and identify specific actions that will get the ball rolling.

To illustrate, let me share a couple of examples from my life at the time of this writing.

In my role as a time management coach, my intention includes reaching and helping as many people as possible live meaningful and rich daily lives. A project that I have taken on to help me fulfill that intention is to write and publish this book. The action plan expanded over several months and included some large tasks (such as designing the cover, finalizing the edits, and implementing a marketing plan), but also more granular tasks for this week (such as revising Part 2, submitting potential cover designs), and completing even more specific tasks for today (post images to Basecamp, enter final edits in master file).

In my role as a family planner, my intention includes our family experiencing new and fun things together. I have taken on an initiative to plan an outdoor activity day, and this week I will propose some dates for our outing.

In my role as the marketing manager for my business, my intention includes "to vibrantly and courageously describe my services to my ideal clients." One initiative I have committed to is that I will create and offer a valuable complementary tool to attract them to sign up for my newsletter! My next action is to select which tool I think would benefit the majority of "my people."

We go from intention to identifying a more specific pursuit that can be translated into action. The goal is never to be productive for the sake of being productive. Rather, we want to be productive for the sake of fulfilling our intentions.

Less Busy *With* and More Busy *Why*

Productivity can be highly overrated. Although I've always been driven to be efficient and ensure the maximum outcome of whatever I was doing, I've come to realize that we often mistake the goal of productivity to be the goal itself. Even when I volunteered at the food bank, packing rice with a group of other volunteers, I couldn't control my urge to maximize the efficiency of our little assembly line. We teamed up on a mini production line to scoop rice from a large bin into approximately one-pound plastic bags, then weigh the bags and add/remove some granules so that, in fact, it was one-pound exactly. We'd then seal bags, put on a label, and pack fifteen of them into a cardboard box which was then stacked on a pallet.

Do you think I just took my spot and went with the flow . . . ? No, of course not. I started instinctively looking for how we could move more finished rice boxes onto the pallet, preferably faster than the people on the assembly line right next to us. I saw that the "weight person" was removing rice from some bags and adding to others. I realized that it would be quicker if the bags were always slightly *underfilled* and that she'd always *add* a little until the scale showed one pound. I realized that since the sealer machine was a limiting factor for how fast that person could go, it would make more sense if someone else applied the labels. In my eagerness to increase our efficiency, I realize (in hindsight) that I probably stressed everyone out. By jumping in to refill the stack of plastic bags *just* before it was out, grabbing an extra set of labels, or doing whatever I noticed would soon be needed, I lost connection to the bigger purpose. The foodbank is a nonprofit organization and volunteering is available for people of different skills and a desire to actually do hard work. They need individuals to volunteer their time, and they want us to keep showing up for these packing events. I do realize that my skill can be very useful; however, it's a fine line— providing this "go-getter" approach and inspiration *and* knowing when it is too intense for others. If I, at that time, had been more connected to my own intention as a volunteer (finding enjoyable ways to leverage my resources in doing good for others) as well as the overall intention of the program, I would have approached it with more lightness and made more of a connection with my fellow volunteers.

Any time we get too "heads down" and focused on just getting things done, we risk getting disconnected from what truly matters about the activity or project in the first place. If we invite friends over for an enjoyable evening and we end up spending most of our time stressing out about hosting rather than truly spending time with our friends, perhaps we would do better to organize it differently. As Priya Parker shares in her brilliant book *Why We Gather*, if we want to fulfill a certain intention (with a gathering), it is essential to keep our primary objective front and center throughout the whole process. It starts with the invitation, the way we prepare our guests for the event, the way we set up the space, the activities we plan . . . and goes all the way to how we connect after the event.

When we plan our time while guided by the meaningful intentions we have set for certain parts of our lives, our chances of ending up feeling satisfied and fulfilled increases by leaps and bounds. It will help us say "yes" to what truly matters and "no" (or "perhaps later") to what doesn't.

By using such a deliberate approach, we can live our lives *today* in a way that feels fulfilling, on purpose, and authentically ours. That way our *daily* life becomes a reflection of how we want to live our life overall.

One motto I try to live by is that "I plan to live to 100 and aim to live each day as if I will." There are definitely activities I prioritize today that are not what I most enjoy or would prefer giving my time to, but as I imagine myself in the future, it becomes clear why I choose to invest that way in myself today.

When I *plan* to live to 100, I know I will need to take good care of my body, starting today. When I plan to live to 100 and make a significant contribution in my lifetime to society, I know I need to find ways to work toward that great contribution, starting now. I will do what I can to honor each day by being in alignment with that vision.

If I want to be healthy and content at 100, I need to consider: What do I need to start doing now? I know that if I focus each day on making progress toward a meaningful goal, and on how I am growing my capacity to eventually and fully accomplish a dream, I can enjoy the journey and reach my goals. I can find satisfaction in honoring what matters to me and receive each seemingly "failed" experiment as a teaching moment. Each pursued action has the potential to teach me something about what I value, and each avoidance can bring awareness to what I am afraid of.

When we can think of time—each month, week, day, and even every moment—as being a mini version of our lives, and aim to align our actions and our way of showing up with how we want to live that life, each segment of time can feel rich and meaningful.

It might feel tempting to think that *"Right now* is not a good time,"* and that "I will *definitely* put something into action as soon as_____ (whatever currently takes much of your energy and attention) is done." Please do not wait until later, until some point when "such and such" is in place. Our lives are "in progress" right now and our lives will always be "works-in-progress." It is now that we have the opportunity to understand ourselves better, and let that awareness inform the choices we make in our daily lives. Those daily choices in turn put us on that path of living a truly fulfilling life. In fact, I believe that the way we live our days is the way we end up living our lives. Let's choose carefully!

Planning Versus Doing Modes

The long game of intentions, setting goals, and defining projects is essential in setting our direction. Yet it's what we do in each moment, the actual actions we take, that moves us toward those goals.

When we learn how to frequently "zoom out" to reconnect with the big picture, and again "zoom in" to take appropriate action, we can infuse each day with more of what matters to us.

In order to effectively switch modes from big picture imagining and envisioning to action-oriented mode, it is useful to know that our brain actually has two main ways of functioning. As explained by Ann Betz (expert on the intersection of neuroscience, coaching, and human transformation), we have a "task-positive" network (for focused doing), and a "default mode" network (for envisioning and planning). When we engage the "task-positive" network, the focus is on the action and getting things done. For planning and big-picture visioning, we instead need to engage the more dreamy "default" network.

When we are unaware of this or think we can do both simultaneously, we risk ending up frustrated with a sense that we are just spinning our wheels.

So how do we consciously engage one or the other mode? First of all, it helps to have this awareness and make it a deliberate choice to enter either action mode (task-positive network, what I call zoom in), or the broader mode connected to envisioning and planning (default network, what I call zoom out). Since our culture and habits are likely to reward action, most of us need to be especially deliberate in allowing ourselves time and space to zoom out. It's often easier to just go with all the demands that end up on our lap from others rather than deliberately plan our focus. Planning does not give the same instant reward; it does not satisfy the need or urge of "getting-things-done." Therefore, we need to give attention to how we set up our space—to entice us to envision and dream, remove distracting to-do lists, and eliminate any other possible temptations that will lure us back into action mode.

Bias toward Action

Nearly every Monday morning, I am tempted to just "dive in" and start *doing* whatever calls my attention as needing to get done. At that moment it feels more productive to start my week with action rather than start by pausing and planning.

When the demands on our time and attention seem endless, of course it is tempting to get into action immediately. After all, we long to have those tasks out of the way, the demands met, and the to-do list items checked off. We know it all needs to get done, so why waste time planning and prioritizing? Let's have a look at what tends to happen when we aren't deliberate in our prioritization of our work, our tasks, and, really, our life.

The problem is multifold; we might start "plugging away" on tasks that feel like quick wins and end up using much of our energy and time on low-priority work. When we just tackle whatever demand screams the loudest, we lose our connection to our bigger goals. At the end of the day, or the week, or the year(!), we feel like we are still just plugging away, barely scratching the surface of *all* that we would like to get done.

It's important to understand that, biologically, planning and prioritization demands a lot of us. "Prioritizing is one of the brain's most energy-hungry processes," says David Rock in his book *Your Brain at Work*. He goes on to point out the complexity of prioritization and how it involves every function: "Understanding new ideas, making decisions, remembering and inhibiting, all at once. It's like the triathlon of mental tasks."

Due to this, it is important to prioritize at an optimal time, when we are fresh, have limited distractions, and can set ourselves up to succeed.

It serves us to consider when during the week and when during the day it is best for us to do our prioritization. In order to set ourselves up for success, it is also advisable to make prioritization into a routine. When we make it a habit to set aside the same time slot each week to plan, and do this at a time when our mind is fresh, we lessen the friction. To get ready for a triathlon we'd put in a lot of training hours, but in the immediate hours before the race, we'd avoid any physical exertion in order to perform at our best. Likewise, when we prioritize on a larger scale, we can make sure we have not already exhausted our mental capacities by other conceptual or analytical thinking. We want to set up our environment so that we are not distracted, and are less likely to have our attention diverted to "shiny objects. We might turn off notifications on our phones and alert colleagues or family that we are not to be disturbed during the coming half-hour (or whatever time you want to protect).

Now that you know how energy-consuming prioritization is, how action-biased we are, and the significantly different modes of action versus envisioning in which we can engage, it's time to apply this knowledge in a more practical sense. In the next segments, I will introduce the core part of my approach: Dump–Divide–Do.

Whether we are proactively planning out our tasks based on our intentions, or we need help to get off the hamster wheel of "crazy busy," we can use this same approach. It will help us get into a more sane space of clear expectations and set a sustainable pace.

Ideally, we want to find space and time to work on our top-down planning where we let our intentions inform our plan as if we are starting with an empty slate. Although that is very rarely the case, I want to first share this ideal approach so that you see how it all fits together. When we feel overwhelmed, frazzled, or spread too thin, we are likely to take the easy path. It's human, it's natural, no need to be hard on ourselves, as when we are exhausted we simply don't have the capacity or willpower to rise above "getting by." When we are stretched too thin, we are less likely to have the discipline to stick to our commitments and stay connected to the big picture and our ultimate goals. Of course, we don't make good decisions when we are in an overwhelmed state. Rock likens it to a chaotic stage. When we have too many "actors" (demands/priorities) on our mental stage, the easy path might be to speed up and frantically try to keep up anyway. Or, we might pick one random action—a relatively manageable one—to work on, and ignore the rest of what's going on. The key is to calm our mind enough, call in the "stage director," and make some conscious choices, rather than randomly and frantically grabbing something to do.

Once when I was on a trip to the beautiful Hawaiian island of Kauai, we headed out on a boat to go scuba diving. The seas were a bit rough and by the time we got our gear on and jumped into the water, I had already started feeling seasick. I felt claustrophobic in my heavy gear, the waves were splashing my face. Our divemaster indicated that it was time to go under, but every cell of my body was resisting the idea of taking water over my head under these conditions. She came up to me, loosened my BCD vest slightly so that I could breathe better, and said, "It's calm down there. Just come down below the surface." My pulse is increasing even now as I recall this story, but I also remember the relief

I felt when I descended below the rough waves and entered into the magical and gorgeous calm of the waters below me.

I'm telling you this story here because I think that, in many ways, it is the same feeling when we are overwhelmed and spread thin with the demands, projects, and responsibilities in our life. It feels completely counterintuitive to stop and feel the calm that is actually available to us, just a few deep breaths away. It only takes a few minutes of engaging in the process of Dump and Divide to regain confidence that we can handle this.

Go from Overwhelmed to Focused Action

Reasons to Dump-Divide-Do:

- To proactively plan our time according to our intentions (ideal scenario)
- To become less overwhelmed, scattered, unclear, when facing too many demands
- To manage being overly ambitious and thereby overcommitted (but with clarity)

Let's start with the ideal approach of proactively planning our action based on our inspired intentions! If you cannot create the headspace to consider this ideal scenario, head over to the section Bottoms-up Approach for Dump-Divide-Do for a different version of the same approach.

Dump

Even this top-down approach can be used for multiple reasons. We might flesh out an action plan for a particular initiative or project, or for a specific area of our life (one of our roles).

You'll need:

- A pencil
- A stack of sticky notes
- One large (poster-size) paper or several A4/letter-size papers

If you have a kanban board, you can use that instead of paper. A kanban board is essentially a grid in which your tasks will flow from left to right. The main purpose is to ensure you limit how many tasks are allowed in each column as a way to ensure that flow.

> **Note:** My preferred way is to work with sticky notes because they are both tactile and movable. I recommend using the smaller size (2" x 1.5" or ~5 x 3.5 cm). The bigger version works as well, but you will need a bigger surface on which to place them.

The first step is to *Dump*, and although it might sound like we'll be putting it all in the bin, we are not actually throwing anything out yet. The goal here is to get all those potential to-dos *out of our heads and onto paper.*

Pick one of the initiatives you identified in the Mind The Gap chapter. Preferably, start with one that you feel some energy around. For this specific initiative or area of your life, write down every to-do item that you can think of, placing each item on a separate sticky note. Set a timer for five minutes and start writing. Keep writing any and every to-do that you can think of, in *no particular order.*

Place the stickies randomly onto your blank sheet of paper. Some of the tasks might be tiny, some might be huge, and that's OK. Some might be super specific, some might be vague, and that's OK too. Some are obvious, some obscure and unclear. The point here is to empty our busy minds, just as if we would dump all the contents of our purse onto a table. Some random things might fall out. Some things that we didn't even know were in there will fall out. At this point in the process, it is important to avoid the temptation to sort, assess, and prioritize. The goal here is just to get it all *out of your head* and onto paper.

For example, for my initiative to write this book, I initially wrote down plenty of large tasks, such as: *Find "my" editor, Create an outline,* and

Decide on the title. I also captured some smaller ones, such as: *Check if URL is available, Talk to Sue about her experience.*

Some tasks were still fuzzy, such as: *Figure out how to publish,* and some really specific: *Send a thank you note to Jennifer.*

At this point, try to keep the floodgates open and just pour out all the potential to-dos until you feel like most of them are written, each on a separate sticky note, then keep going another couple of minutes! Make sure everything you can think of at this time is "out on paper."

The process of letting all those thoughts get out and onto paper will not only free up lots of mental space, but it will also give you clarity about your level of clarity!

At this point, it is possible that your initiative feels overwhelming. Hang in there, we are not through yet.

Divide

Once your sticky-note writing is done, at least for now, it's time to create some order in the madness. To do so, you will divide your tasks in two different ways: by time, and by size.

Divide - By Time

For this second step of the process, I recommend a more specific structure than in other parts of the book. Once you have tried it and understand the purpose behind it, feel free to adjust exactly how you do this according to your preferences.

If you're starting with blank sheets, go ahead and draw a six-column grid, allowing each column to be *at least* the width of a sticky note. Alternatively, use a separate A4/Letter-size paper for each column.

LATER	THIS MONTH	THIS WEEK	TODAY	DOING	DONE

At this point it might seem counterintuitive that the columns move from Later on the left, to Today on the right, but please stick with it. It will all make sense soon.

Initially, our Doing and Done columns will be blank. Only once we have *committed* to our plan for the week, we'll get into Doing. But before we do, we need to create a realistic plan and increase our chances of achieving our goals.

What you'll do next is to take one sticky note/task at a time, from your dumped to-dos and determine: *When* do I need (or want) to **start** doing this? Today, this week, later this month, even later? If it is something you need to start today, put it in the Today column. If it is something you need to start this week or this month, put it in the appropriate column. If it's something you don't need to start until next month, put it in the Later column.

Make sure you decide pretty quickly, without overthinking (there will be plenty of opportunities to fine-tune later). Continue, one stickie at a time, until you've grouped them all by *when* to start. Depending on how many stickies you dumped, this will likely take only a couple of minutes.

Double-check that any tasks in the This Month or Later columns really do not require *any* action on your part *this* week. If they do, add new stickies in the This Week column to reflect the specific action you need to take sooner.

Divide - By Size

Now some good news: Anything that is further out on our time horizon (This Month or Later) can now be considered "parked." We don't need to do anything else about those at this time, because we don't need a more granular level of detail for those tasks or projects yet. At a later point in the process, we will revisit those tasks and divide by size as they become more imminent.

For anything in the Today or This Week columns, however, we will do a further divide and separate out those to-dos into more specific, small-action steps. Now, take one stickie from your Today column. Pick it up and consider it closely. Ask yourself, "When do I need to **complete** this task?" You might realize at this point that certain aspects need to be completed today, whereas others can wait until later in the week, or even later in the month. If so, replace the original sticky with multiple smaller tasks to indicate what you will *complete* when. When you're done with one sticky note, pick up another and repeat the process until all tasks in the Today and This Week columns reflect what needs to be completed within those timeframes.

I suggest you write your tasks using a verb + a noun: *Call Maria, Pay bill.* It will often include a further detail or description: *Call Maria about proposal, Email Steven about payment, Select photo for blog post.* The key is to make the action item precise enough that you will know exactly what to do, yet keep it short and concise.

For a writing project, here are some of the tasks I ended up with for Today and This Week: *Draft blog post, Find photo for blog, Review/revise blog, Publish blog.*

Repeat this process of dividing by time and by size for any other initiatives you are ready to put into action. The goal here is to reach a point when what we have on our Today and This Week "plate" feels doable. Our head is clear and we are ready for some Focused Action!

Before we dive into action I want to share a few more tips for how to define tasks that set you up for success.

How Small Is Small Enough?

I recommend you aim to have most action items be small enough to be completed in an hour or less. The reason is that, for the most part, human beings have a hard time focusing on something for much longer than that. In neuroscience, we learn about ultradian rhythms—a biological inner rhythm that lasts about ninety minutes. Research has shown that after about ninety minutes of focused work, the neurochemicals required for focus actually start diminishing. At that time, we are better off shifting to another activity or, better yet, getting some rest.

One Sitting - One Focus (Our *Very* Limited Capacity to Multitask)

Although we are not yet at a place to get into action, I find it important to already bring your attention to just how bad we are at multitasking. For the most part, when we think we are multitasking, we are really *switching* focus a lot between different tasks. Such task switching is energy intensive for our brain since we keep shifting the context and need to re-enter each activity over and over again. The only time we can truly do more than one thing at a time is when one of the activities is reflexive, i.e., so ingrained and automatic that it doesn't require our conscious attention. Most of us can walk and chew gum at the same time! You can drive your regular route to work while listening to the radio, but perhaps you've noticed that when you have to drive in a more complex situation, like finding your way in a new and busy city, you need to turn the radio off because you now need to give your full attention to finding your way.

It's also important to realize that the task-switching we engage in when we think we are multitasking is both energy- and time-consuming. When we find ourselves scattered across too many priorities, we are better off stopping to recalibrate.

For all those reasons, I suggest you break down your bigger tasks into something you will be able to complete in one sitting. That way, if you set yourself up to complete them without having your attention diverted, you will be more likely to stick with the task until you are done. For things that require more than one sitting, or for some reason seem best to separate out, put them on separate sticky notes. Some stickies might stay in the Today column, and some might move out to This Week or This Month, or even Later.

How Will I Know I'm Done?

When we plan our time, it is important to specify what we commit to. Part of the planning process is to review and reconnect with our goals and intentions, and to determine what specific activities we will take on in the upcoming timeframe—be it the next year, season, month, week, day, or even hour. When we have large initiatives that span several weeks, it is essential to clarify specifically what will be *completed* in the next time period.

One effective way to set yourself up to succeed is to get very clear and up-front about what criteria you will use to consider the task (or project) done. When we work on dividing our big tasks or projects into actionable tasks, it can be useful to engage the concept of Done criteria. The Done criteria essentially answers the question: How will I know I'm done? When we proactively take the time to determine the criteria that need to be met in order to complete the task or project milestone, we can more easily set ourselves up to succeed. That clarity makes it possible to set expectations with both ourselves and others, and avoid the unnecessary stress that comes with trying to live up to impossible expectations.

The Done criteria for a task answers the question: What, very specifically, will I have completed before checking this item off my to-do list? We can also define Done criteria for larger goals or milestones. In that case, the question will be similar: How will I know that I have arrived at the milestone? How will I know that this goal has been accomplished?

The specificity of a Done criteria will help us on a daily basis in a couple of ways:

1. Rather than having a poorly defined task "in progress" day after day (and maybe even week after week), break it down into distinguishable and completable tasks that can be checked off as we take action and make progress.

2. Rather than getting frustrated or disillusioned about the seeming lack of progress due to a vaguely defined task, a clear definition of Done will both make it very clear when we are done, and will also allow us to own the accomplishment and perhaps even celebrate our progress.

One such example for me is planning our family summer travels. With family spread across multiple countries and different wants and needs of each family member, this planning is quite an undertaking and it can be hard to get a sense of progress each week. So, rather than having a task that says "plan summer trip," which is work-in-progress for weeks on end, I determine a specific Done criteria for "plan summer trip" each week. This week I will have researched flight prices for scenario X, I will have asked my sister about her holiday plans, and found out when my son's school ends. I know what I am taking on and, at the end of the week, I can feel a sense of accomplishment! Next week I define other tasks that will gradually help me complete our plan for the summer.

How to Be Crisp When Outcome Is Vague

Sometimes we need to choose more ambiguous Done criteria on purpose. Yet, even a vague objective like seeing what comes out of a brainstorming session needs to have a specific goal. The goal can still be specific in the sense that we have selected a topic to do brainstorming around and we have a desired outcome (ideas about challenge X, potential solutions to problem Y). In addition, it's good to be deliberate about what format and method we'll use to support that goal (facilitate brainstorming, discuss, capture all ideas, etc.). When we set expectations with ourselves or our collaborators about what we will focus on, we clarify what the desired outcome is.

With specified Done criteria, we also have a better chance of *estimating* the work required because it forces us to think about the pieces that are necessary to reach that completed state. Once we have the tasks broken down, we are likely to estimate better.

When we set clear Done criteria for our tasks and milestones, we also clarify *what will NOT be done*, at least not right now. By distinguishing what's "in" and what's "out, we can communicate expectations with others. In some cases, a negotiation might be required about what will be "good enough for now."

Having a crisp definition about when we will reach our sub-goals will also *help us stay focused on the tasks* that will actually contribute to that completion. No more scattering our attention across *all* the tasks that need to be completed for the bigger goal. In addition, a clear Done criteria for our sub-goals will give us the opportunity to, and satisfaction of, *marking tasks and milestones as complete* along the way to that bigger goal. Chunks of work can be marked as completed and hopefully already provide value, rather than having the whole big project "in progress" for a long, long time.

We're almost there . . . but before we dive into the final part of this process—actually *doing* the tasks—there is one more check. Ask yourself:

*Considering **other** commitments and current **circumstances**, does what I have listed to complete This Week seem achievable without unnecessary stress?*

Four More D's

What if I'm *still* overwhelmed?

So, all your tasks/stickies have been separated out by time and then also broken down into smaller pieces for anything that must be completed in the short term.

If you still feel overwhelmed at this point, it might serve you to consider another four D's to come up with a realistic plan:

1. Delay
2. Delegate
3. Divide (further)
4. Drop

Looking at each of the stickies you have on your board, in your Today column (or Week—whatever timeframe feels overwhelming), assess if you can reduce your load and come up with an action plan to get the most important work done using these four D actions:

Delay

For anything not truly urgent, consider deferring those tasks to a later time. With everything you have going on right now, perhaps you need to defer some of these pieces. Consider what expectations you need to (re)set as a result, and be sure to communicate with others who might be affected by the delay.

Delegate

Alternatively, you might choose to look to someone else to support you in getting some tasks done, if they truly need to get done. You might delegate or ask for help. Consider: How can I get these somewhat important things done by using other resources? How can I tap into someone else's capacity or brilliance in order to complete these tasks?

Divide—Further

It can also be useful to take another look at the size of your tasks and consider if there is an aspect of the commitment that is very urgent and if other parts can wait. If so, separate out the task by when each piece truly needs to be completed. What will have to be *good enough* for now? What *part* of this is truly urgent?

Drop

Perhaps you realize that, in the bigger scheme of things, some tasks are really not that important. For anything that is neither important nor urgent, but seems more like a nice-to-have, consider whether those tasks are even worthy of your time. What "bad thing" might happen if you don't do them?

Keep working through these additional four D's until you feel that your plan for the Week feels doable.

No matter which of these additional four D's you utilize, it is likely you will also need to reset expectations with others who are involved or affected by your decision. Make sure to reach out to avoid misunderstandings and increased complexities later on.

Before you DO, Commit, Consider: How Realistic Is My Plan?

By now I'm guessing you are eager to dive into action. Let's do this!

You have clarified all your to-dos, in addition to getting really precise about the Done criterion for each to-do. Great! One final preparation is very important for setting yourself up for success and not overcommitting.

Sometimes we have an increasing feeling that we will not be able to actually do all that we have listed for ourselves. Without initially realizing it, there is an inner anxiety that builds up because on some level we know that we cannot complete all those tasks in that amount of time. Although we have a strong feeling that these are all important tasks and cannot take them off our list, we are not letting any other tasks budge either. We get stuck in the unrealistic pursuit, and just hope that it will somehow resolve itself. In order to set ourselves up for success, it is important to be realistic and honest with ourselves when committing. We need to set expectations with ourselves and with others about what we can actually complete in a given period of time.

A Caution about Overcommiting and Undercommitting

This is a good time to remind ourselves that we tend to overestimate what we can do in a day or a week, but *underestimate* what we can do in a year or five years. Overcommitting in the short term is easy to do when we get pumped up and ambitious. When we feel like our to-do list is chasing us, we tend to overcommit to what we can do in a day. We optimistically fill up our calendars for the week without taking into consideration that we'll probably get more tasks and demands added as we go. At the end of the day, or week, we end up feeling like we never get enough done.

When they first come to me, most of my clients are in the habit of taking on too much due to expectations and beliefs about what they *should* be doing. I invite them, and you, to "question reality" and dig a bit deeper to explore the shoulds in your life, and, really, in your mind.

- "I should get more done in a day." Really?
- "I should be further along than I am." Is that absolutely true?
- "I should have a stronger social media presence." Says who? What would that do for you or your business?

What if these were not true, or at least not the whole truth? Throughout the remaining pages, you'll get to discover how people, places, situations, and tasks affect you and experiment to find ways that specifically fit you. You'll get to try an approach of curiosity and experimentation. You can then choose either to stay head-down and follow the path you're on with the imposed "rules," or you can truly *own* your life and align "the work" with what fulfills you.

One day recently, I found myself feeling overwhelmed and task-switching, dibbling and dabbling, having a super hard time getting focused. I felt frustrated that I wasn't making much progress on anything.

All the important pieces were in place:

- I had set clear and inspired goals.
- My goals were aligned with my bigger intentions and values.
- My daily actions were clearly supporting me in accomplishing those goals.

In other words; I knew what I wanted and I was "going after it"!

Somehow, I had gotten overambitious and committed to too much. As exciting and inspiring as it was to get momentum on those most-inspired goals, I had to remind myself that there are only so many hours in a day, and only so much I can keep in focus at one given time. I paused and, like I often do, took my own medicine. I considered what was most essential that I focus on today, and what would need to be delayed. I reminded myself that I could accomplish more if I narrowed my focus and truly gave my attention to one thing at a time.

The key to making significant progress on our really big goals is to stick to them over time. Pick a select few, truly important larger initiatives and stay in action. Keep doing something. A single daily action over three years means more than 1,000 steps toward our dream. Even a monthly action/habit of doing something—let's say making a painting—will leave us with thirty-six paintings in those three years—enough to have an exhibition!

We've got to break down those bigger important goals in a way that they can fit within our life. Rather than putting those important long-term life goals aside to gather dust, we need to find ways to do them in some form and stay in action, moving toward our dreams, however gradual or minimal.

Do

Remember that "task mode" that we have in our brain? Well, now is its time to shine. It is time to get out of our envisioning and dreaming "default mode" and focus our attention on specific tasks. It is time to put the blinders on and remove any distractions.

At the beginning of each day, do a quick Daily Planning. Consider the tasks you've committed to under the Week column, and move the stickies that you commit to *complete* today into the Today column.

All other tasks are considered "parked" and can be kept **out of sight** *and out of mind until your next Daily Planning.* Do what you can to minimize distractions and actually stay focused on the tasks you have committed to. Do not attempt to multitask!

Once you have planned your day and have assessed how realistic your commitment is, it's time to get into action! Take one of the stickies from Today and move that into the Doing column. Ideally, from this point forward, you want to have only one task at a time in Doing, or work-in-progress. Stick with this one task until it is done. Once done, move that sticky all the way over to the Done column and give yourself a high-five for staying focused and making progress on your commitments!

Create a Parking Lot/Wear Your Blinders

In the Divide section, I emphasized breaking down your action into small enough pieces to be done in one sitting. That clarity is intended to help you focus on one thing at a time.

As we get into action, it is essential to limit work-in-progress. In other words, once you start something, you'll keep your attention on that until you finish it. If you have broken down your action to be small enough to do in one sitting, this is going to be much easier. When you limit the number of items you put in the Doing column (ideally just one), you also avoid the temptation to task-switch and be distracted by all the other tasks that are lingering.

As you dive in to do your work, your committed tasks, you will likely have distractions. Thoughts and ideas about other work will pop up and you will need to have a way to get them out of your head and "parked."

For this reason, it's very useful to create a "parking lot" in which you capture any fleeting or nagging thoughts about other actions you need to take. That way you can quickly jot down those thoughts or ideas and come right back to your committed work. In order for you to really let go of those distracting thoughts, you need to trust that the parking lot *will* be reviewed. Later in the process you'll see how the parking lot gets brought back into your next planning session. That's when you will make deliberate choices about what gets priority and when each will be done.

Make sure your parking lot is easily accessible, yet out of sight. It needs to be accessible enough so that you can easily add notes, yet out of sight enough so it won't attract your attention.

Done

Finally, perhaps the most satisfactory step of them all, as we complete a task, is to move it to our Done column. Check it off. Do a happy dance. "Rinse and repeat" until Today's tasks have all been completed!

At the end of the day, acknowledge yourself for what you have accomplished!

In our high-intensity work environments and "speedy" society, we tend to skip by the moment of really feeling success. Even for larger accomplishments, we tend to just check tasks off as done and keep moving on to the next project and the next . . . and the next. No wonder many of us feel that our to-do lists seem like bottomless pits!

I hope to inspire you to define and celebrate success not only for your larger goals but also for the steps that lead toward an ultimate goal. Eventually, we can reach all our juicy goals. But, unless we find a way to clone ourselves multiple times over and put the rest of the world on pause, we surely cannot reach them all today.

Each deliberate choice leads to self-empowerment. Each time we feel a sense of progress, we boost our self-confidence.

Imagine if most of our time was invested in inspired, focused action. How much could we accomplish of what truly matters? What would happen to our sense of fulfillment?

Now *Is* the Best Time

I hope you are starting to see how your clarity about what deeply matters to you can inform your action planning and, essentially, how you invest your time. You might not see transformation overnight, but by honoring your dreams and taking *some* action, you are overcoming the challenge of "never enough time" and "I'll get to it someday" and are starting to live those intentions. By taking deliberate action, step by step, day by day, you gradually empower yourself to live those dreams.

Remember the exercise of identifying the gap between the ideal state as described in your intention and your current level of living into that intention? Well, sometimes we put off starting, because we keep waiting until sometime "soon" when we will have more time. We tell ourselves, "Soon I will feel more ready" or "Once other things have settled down, I'll *definitely* start," but that time seems to perpetually get pushed out. Rather than waiting for some "perfect" moment to finally start, I recommend finding *something you can* do. It might be tiny steps, progress in tiny little doses, but start *now*. If you want to paint, give yourself a little scribble time, draw with your kids, use colorful pens to take notes at work, add little visuals or designs as part of your note-taking. Find ways to start to incorporate those dreams and desires in your life right now.

- How can I accomplish even a small version of living into my intention *this week*?
- What can I do *today* that gives me some of the feelings I've indicated in my intention?

If we connect with the essence of what we want, what the experience or feeling is that we are after, it gets easier to find ways to start incorporating that essence, even in small ways, in our daily lives.

If we long for a vacation but know we cannot take one for a while, we can consider what *specifically* about that vacation we are longing for. Perhaps we long for some slow time to just sit and read. Perhaps it has more to do with exploring a brand-new environment. Perhaps we long for some quality time with our family. So, get creative: Consider how to incorporate the essence of that into your everyday life. You might give yourself a few hours on Sunday to just read for pleasure. You might make an outing of visiting a town nearby where you've never been, or be a tourist in your own city for a day. You might plan a game night or a picnic in order to get some yummy time with your family.

Some of us have a "someday dream" about being on a big stage with our message. Take some time to imagine what you'd be *feeling* if you did that. Tap into: What's the essence of what I hope to experience? Then explore what small ways you could experience that now. If you are hoping to inspire the people in that big audience to take action, how could you have that same effect on a smaller group, or perhaps even just one individual, today? If we long to allocate more of our time to program creation, and less to administration, what is a small way to shift our energy toward those tasks, perhaps by simplifying, automating, or outsourcing some of the administrative tasks?

Bottoms-up Approach for Dump-Divide-Do

With the complex and multifaceted lives we live, it's no wonder we sometimes get overwhelmed. The question is, how do we get out of feeling overwhelmed? How do we get into inspired and focused action? As counterintuitive as it is when we are that busy, we actually need to stop, pause long enough to find our footing, and make deliberate choices that reflect our true priorities.

One time while leading a workshop, I took the group through the Dump-Divide-Do process. One woman, Mary, came into the workshop feeling rather overwhelmed, desperately looking for managing all that was on her plate. At her work, she was responsible for several PR projects, managed the company's social media presence, and was in charge of completing an application for a grant. When asked to assess her level of feeling overwhelmed on a scale from one (very low) to ten (very high), she assessed an herself at an eight. During the Dump segment of the exercise, she was writing frenetically, completely filling several sheets of paper with stickies that captured all the actions she needed to take.

Once done with that first step, she felt some relief at having spewed out all those tasks onto paper. When I asked her to again assess her overwhelmed level, she looked at all that she had written, shook her head, and let out a big, defeated sigh. She assessed her level at a ten, saying she felt maxed out and doubted that this exercise would do her any good. It seemed to her, at that moment, like the activity would not fulfill the promise of the workshop: "From Overwhelm to Focused Action." I asked her to take a deep breath and stick with it. As she worked to divide out her tasks over the coming weeks and months, she felt some relief that everything did not need her attention immediately. However, once she divided her tasks by time, she realized just how many to-dos she identified as "must complete" either today or this week. Her anxiety level started to rev up again, when it dawned on her that getting all of that done, without any assistance, was simply not feasible. She took a big breath and said, "I see now. There is no way any one person could do all of that in just a few days." She acknowledged that the expectations were completely out of whack and that she needed to bring this to the management. They would have to make some choices about what was most important and urgent, then divide further (and identify the absolute top-priority aspects), and then delay, delegate, or delete.

Within the brief time of this hour-long workshop, Mary got to a place where she realized that she could speak up and escalate the prioritization to the appropriate level. By getting all the tasks out of her head and sorted by when they needed to happen, it became very obvious that no amount of working harder would make her successful. Finally, she assessed her overwhelm level as "six" and she felt clear about what focused action she needed to take: Have that conversation with her manager.

When we are really busy, stressed out, or overwhelmed, it's easy to just keep pushing harder. It seems counterintuitive to stop for a moment and actually consider what options we have. We attempt to multitask and keep switching focus, then actually end up getting less quality work done. When we are overwhelmed, we tend to get reactive because we are neither grounded nor connected to the broader perspective. We exhaust ourselves by trying to juggle all those to-dos and holding all those "must-not-forgets" in our heads.

It can be useful to know that, according to neuroscience, the mind can only hold very limited information in the prefrontal cortex (the short-term memory bank of the mind). David Rock puts it like this: "There appear to be real limits to the amount of information that can be held in the prefrontal cortex at any one time." It is not energy efficient to try to juggle too many ideas, problems, and concepts in our minds. Rock goes on to describe this short-term memory this way: "Your memory degrades for each item when you hold a lot in mind." That helps us understand why it is helpful to clear out most of what we are trying to store in our short-term memory. It will free up our capacity to resolve gnarly problems, including the energy-intense activity of prioritization.

In Mary's case, all her tasks were clearly related to important initiatives in her work. Sometimes, once we dump, we might need to spend a little time considering how all those to-dos really matter. Are we busy with things that are not in line with our intentions or the intended outcomes of a project? If not, what is actually important about those tasks in the bigger picture?

Two things might happen as a result:

1. We realize that some of our drudgery tasks are actually meaningful, even though the tasks themselves have not changed. Once we make that connection to an important goal, we find them more meaningful.

2. Or, we don't find any connection to something meaningful and we can seriously consider whether these tasks are worthy of our energy and attention. If not, we drop them (and re-set expectations with others as appropriate).

Wasting energy on thoughts that keep recurring in our mind, usually related to what overwhelms us, is another reason to dump. Like clearing out a junk drawer, if we get it all out on the table, we are more likely to be able to see it for what it is and sort it through. Rather than a big jumble in our heads, we now have something to work with.

In the "ideal" scenario (Top-down Dump-Divide-Do), our starting point was either an inspired intention, or an already prioritized initiative. The same process can be used any time we feel either disoriented or overwhelmed. In this case you will approach Dump-Divide-Do with the broader focus of anything-and-everything that's rushing around in your head.

Here are the Dump-Divide-Do steps again, in summary:

1. Dump: Take about five minutes to write down all the to-dos that are circling in your head.

    a. Write one task/to-do/must-not-forget on each sticky note.
    b. Place the stickies in no particular order on a surface in front of you.
    c. Keep going until you notice your busy mind slowing down.

2. Dump: Take about five minutes to write down all the to-dos that are circling in your head.

    a. For anything in This Month or Later, put those aside for now.
    b. For anything in Today or This Week, continue to step 3.

3. Divide - by size: Consider one sticky note at a time—what specifically needs to be completed by when.

    a. Break down the tasks by when each task needs to be completed, possibly replacing the original sticky with multiple new ones.
    b. Place each new sticky in the appropriate timeframe.

4. Do: Look over what you ended up with in Today and This Week and consider if it seems feasible.

    a. If not, consider: further Divide, Delay, Delegate, Delete.
        i. Once you've set yourself up for success, commit to giving your energy and attention to those tasks.
        ii. Remove any distractions and get into Focused Action.

Practice Just-in-Time Planning

Yes, You Can Have it All

At some point it all needs to come together; all your roles, initiatives, and to-dos get integrated. You are, after all, just one person, and you will need to prioritize the "top" to-dos across all your roles. At times, one role might need to take a back seat, and perhaps only some minor "maintenance" tasks will show up on this week's list.

Just like we are not trying to accomplish our life's mission in one particular day, our whole purpose or meaning of life will not reveal itself in one given day, or within one particular situation.

When I was leading a workshop on time management and the participants had worked on prioritizing, a woman in the group raised her hand and commented on how all-consuming she found it to be a mother, wondering how she would be able to find time for all the other projects she wanted to pursue. After hearing a bit about her intention as a mother—what was most important to her in her relation to her son—I asked how that measured up to other priorities in her life at that point. Without a doubt, she exclaimed: "He is the *most* important thing in my life." The point with sharing this story is that, in this time of her life, these few years when her son was young and needed more of her attention might not have been the time to also take on *multiple* other large life initiatives. It was her choice. If she really did want to pursue those other initiatives at that time, she might have to get creative about *how* she could go about doing it while still honoring her intentions as a mother. There are an infinite number of ways in *how* we honor our intention, but only so many hours in a day.

Just like certain years might be focused on certain roles, different seasons might be centered around one role. During my summer trip to my native country of Sweden, it's all about family and friends, and some self-care, but no other roles are invited along on this trip. When it is tax season, my family finance manager role gets center stage. When the end of a year nears, I tend to give extra time to contemplation and big-picture visioning.

Planning: Daily, Weekly, Monthly, Seasonal

Daily Planning

So, let's go into some further detail about how to get ongoing traction on all those tasks that you dumped and divided.

Each morning, ask yourself: What do I *commit* to completing today?

At the start of each day, pull in tasks from the This Week column into Today as a way to commit to the day's actions. This helps you learn to stay focused and actually accomplish what you have committed to.

During your working day, you are likely to think of other/new tasks that you need to take care of. Jot them down on a sticky and consider when the next/first action needs to happen. Then place it in that column. Once you have the task logged and "parked," you no longer need to spend precious brain capacity to remember it. You can trust that you will see it when the time comes to plan the next day, or the next week.

Once you are ready for action, pull one action into Doing, and when it's done, pull it into Done.

At the *end* of each day, if all that you committed to was indeed completed, it's time for a happy dance! If not, take a moment to reflect: Did I commit to too much? Were my tasks and Done criteria unclear? What might I adjust in order to accomplish what I commit to tomorrow? Again, it is time for that happy dance! We will cover this very important process of reflecting in more depth in the next section, Ever-Evolving Experimentation.

Weekly Planning

When you want to plan a new week, consider all the tasks in the This Month column. At this point, you have an additional step. Since you did not yet divide these action items by size, your weekly planning needs to include that step. For each task that you bring in from This Month to This Week, consider what is completable within one sitting. Write new stickies as needed. Aim to break down the task enough so that you can focus on one task at a time once you get into Doing, and avoid trying to multitask by having more than one task in progress. This is also a good time to empty your "Parking Lot" (those tasks that popped into your head when you were focused on something else). At this point you want to make sure that those tasks are put in the appropriate time frame for when they need to be completed.

1. Make sure all your to-dos are captured (dump tasks for any new initiatives).
2. Determine when they need to be done (divide by time), and make them specific and small enough to complete in one sitting (divide by size).
3. Commit to what you will complete this week.

Monthly Planning

When you plan your next month, it's time to go back to Dump and Divide to make sure you have captured the details of all that needs doing in the coming month.

In order to stay aligned with your intentions, make sure to prioritize projects and tasks that help you fulfill those intentions, at least partially, during the coming month.

Seasonal Planning

The same process works for seasonal (or quarterly) planning; you will simply broaden your horizon and consider what main initiatives you will prioritize in the upcoming few months. The broader the time horizon, the less detailed your tasks need to be. With a "just-in-time" planning approach like this, the details get fleshed out when you get closer to taking the particular action.

This focused Dump-Divide-Do approach, coupled with goal setting that is guided by our intentions and that feels truly inspired, will keep us on track when it comes to giving our time to what truly matters on a daily basis.

In the next section, we will elaborate on how to keep fine-tuning based on what works for our specific circumstances. Only you can know what works for you, and the way to find out is to experiment.

Any time you find yourself feeling overwhelmed or scattered across initiatives, go back to Dump-Divide-Do. That will help you get clarity about where to focus your attention and energy first. Bring the next task into Doing. Stay focused on just that one thing until you're done, then move it to the Done column. Rinse-and-repeat until you have completed what you committed to.

Conclusion . . .

Use this approach of just-in-time planning and allow your journey to be a series of experiments from which you learn what is working for you and what is not. I suggest that you adopt this approach of ongoing experimentation. Get into action and let it lead you to an increased awareness that allows you to make more and more informed choices that, in turn, bring the most meaning to you. Occasionally, tips from others fit us perfectly, but more likely we need to apply the approach to our own personality and life situation.

In the next segment, we will dive deep into the most essential aspect of creating a time management system that truly fits you. It includes habits of reflection and a willingness to adapt our approach based on what we discover. It's in this next segment, Ever-Evolving Experimentation, where your deepest insights will surface.

PART 5

Ever-Evolving
Experimentation

"All life is an experiment. The more experiments you make the better."

– Ralph Waldo Emerson

EMBRACE THE JOURNEY

The next main part of this overall approach to time management is all about *reflecting* and *adapting*. We can think of our inspired intentions as our why and our action plan and aligned action as the *what* and *when* that will take us closer to living those intentions. This section is all about *how*—about discovering how to implement an approach that truly fits us.

We will build on and fine-tune our inspired intentions and discover how we might want to adjust our action planning to really set ourselves up for success. In this section, we will cover the importance of continuous learning and experimentation. We will consider why it is essential not just to get into action but also to pause long and frequently enough in order to make more informed choices about how to adjust and keep our process fresh and interesting. With that awareness about what we need, about what's truly most important (not just urgent) and what works best for us personally, we can adopt an approach in which we make frequent adjustments to aim toward where we want to be headed.

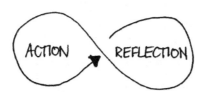

This is a framework of inquiry, through which you get to discover what works for you. You get to create *just* the right structure for you and take the right path for you. The goal is that we make more and more deliberate choices, based on our increased clarity regarding what most matters to us, and what works for us on a very personal level under our current circumstances. We can then take purposeful next steps from which we learn and grow and course-correct.

As stated earlier, by exploring and fine-tuning our paths, and by considering the options we have, we give ourselves the power of choice and let our choices be informed by our intentions and values. The way to gradually get more clarity about your ideal approach is to iterate, experiment, and see what works best for you. We don't know until we try.

Since our circumstances are sure to change over time, as are our preferences, our needs, and wants, it's essential to use a time management approach that is dynamic and assumes nothing remains static. With a process that helps us regularly assess and course-correct, we can make sure that we are always headed where we actually want to be going.

If we were to head straight east from Washington, D.C., over the Atlantic Ocean toward Europe, only a few degrees difference in our course would land us either in Portugal, Spain, or Morocco. If we instead keep checking our course and adjust for currents, drift, wind shifts, etc. and even reassess our goal, we can ensure that we end up at our desired destination.

Frequently Assess and Adjust

In order to reflect, we want to step out of task mode and into a broader focus where we can see how it all connects and fits together. Taking the time to truly listen to someone's answer is one of the biggest gifts we can give someone; truly and deeply listen to how someone else feels. It's an equally big gift, to ourselves, to listen deeply within for answers. A simple but profound question we can ask ourselves is, "How am I?"

If we want to implement sustainable and efficient time management in our lives, we need to learn to stop long enough to listen to ourselves.

If we are constantly pushing forward without any consideration for what actually works for us personally, we will be heading toward either giving up, regretting, or burning out. If we, on the other hand, want to implement ways to use our precious time to fill our soul that uniquely fit us, we need to allow some time to check in with ourselves. To discover a dynamic and ever-evolving approach, we need to be willing to pause and ask ourselves:

- "What's working and what's not?"
- "What do I want or need right now?"
- "What's an adjustment I want to make that will make it more likely that I succeed?"

Make Reflection a Habit

In order to align our daily life closer and closer with what deeply and truly matters to us, we need to reflect and then courageously make decisions and take action, even when the action goes "against the grain," is unexpected, or stirs the pot. Intentional living means that we take responsibility for our lives and we do it with self-compassion. It can feel like a radical act.

When we stop more often and reflect, we can make more deliberate choices. It's useful to reflect yearly and weekly for sure, but there are also daily, monthly, and seasonal reflections. Without this kind of reflection, we risk getting stuck in a rut or blindly following someone else's approach. In order for these reflections to be meaningful, they need to be sincere and honest. We do not need to be the "good student" or the one who has it all figured out. In fact, when we feel like we have to show up as the "A student," we miss out, as we are less likely to courageously look into the spaces that are not yet quite figured out, the places that hold the promise of real learning.

Creating a Sustainable Pace. Indefinitely.

The problem with many time management and productivity approaches is that they are so focused on getting more done and becoming more productive, they lose connection to what we really want to create or experience in this precious lifetime. Often, we approach time management by putting more and more pressure on ourselves to produce more, be more productive, and deliver more, without any significant sense of meaning or satisfaction. What's the point? Sure, we can sacrifice by pushing through in the short term for someone else's goal, but if we don't take care of ourselves and feed ourselves on a soul level, it will not be sustainable. This pushing through has us eat into our reservoir, and if we don't equally replenish it, we will feel more and more worn out by the day. We sacrifice our short-term well-being. Our energy might last a little longer thanks to our determination and drive, but at some point, it is not sustainable. We end up using more energy than we generate, tapping into our reserves, and running on empty.

Let's explore that scenario—one where we sacrifice our short-term well-being for a larger goal. In the worst case, this goal is someone else's and we are just doing the work for them—like when we work for a corporation and its mission is not aligned with our values and our mission. We put in endless hours and all our energy into something we don't care about, or put too much time (without boundaries) into something we do care about, and all we get in return is a paycheck. We might also be honing our skills and learning on the job, but the net result in the short term is that we are slowly burning out, tapping into our reserve.

Over time, our energy—our resource bank—needs to at least be replenished and, ideally, we fill it up way above the minimum level. When we do, we can let that additional energy further boost our inspiration to pursue our dream goals.

Sure, we can do short spurts of using more energy or resources than we actually have available and go into a deficit. If the deficit is temporary and not too deep, we can recover. A sustainable approach has a broader reach and considers the use of both energy and resources over time. It's a holistic view where we ensure we recharge at least as much as we use, and only rarely and temporarily dip into our reserve.

The Potential of Being a Work-in-Progress

I hear many people complain about getting older, dreading another birthday, and I suspect many are afraid of becoming old in the sense that they stagnate in their growth and become less and less capable. I find it useful to consider the alternative. If I am no longer here to have a birthday, to experience another year, it would mean that my life is over. My father lived to be only forty. Oh, do I wish he could be in my life as an old man now. We can put our focus back on what we *still* get to experience, thanks to the fact that we are here and are growing older.

As we progress on our big, important life ambitions, it can feel frustrating when they seem out of reach. At the same time, we realize that if they were easy to reach, the goal would not be as satisfying, and we'd probably already have reached it.

I suggest you *celebrate* the fact that you will never be done, and adopt a mindset of continuous experimentation and evolution.

Much of the work we take on as entrepreneurs, thought leaders, and change-makers is ambiguous. Any time we pursue a really ambitious goal, we are sure to head into uncharted territory! Just like the early maps that were not fully drawn because part of the territory truly was unknown, we are now adventurers on the uncharted territory of our future.

Discovery and adjustments along the way are to be expected. Each new week we get to choose which specific tasks to commit to. When we then get into action mode, start doing, and subsequently learn from that doing, we can gradually fill in the blanks on that map.

Not only am I continuously figuring out this business owner thing, but I also keep exploring improved approaches to time management, and I am still figuring out how I can show up as brilliantly and fully as possible in this one precious life of mine!

And I hope we are never "done." Let's put on our learner hats, add a good sprinkle of curiosity, and dive in to fully engage with whatever is next!

Growth Mindset

The book *Mindset* by Carol Dweck suggests that we take on a *growth mindset*. The way it relates here is that we set the expectation within ourselves that we will have an upward-facing curve of growth. Currently, we have a certain level of skill or knowledge and our intention is to keep growing, getting more skilled, mastering new tasks, and building on our strengths. There will be scary things to try and learn from, forever and ever. There is no externally set "bar" that we are trying to live up to. The only measure is that our growth, our capacity, our skill, our intelligence, our creativity—whatever it is that we want to grow, is pointing upward. If we stagnate, we need to reconsider how we are living our life. Aim for better today than yesterday. Aim for being further along your desired life journey this year than you were last year. The extent to which I know myself and align my life with what's meaningful is fuller each day. Rather than thinking that we are *supposed* to know, we need to embrace being on this journey. We keep trimming those sails and course-correcting to go in the direction we want to end up.

A New Comfort Zone, Yet Always Expanding

With increased self-awareness, over time our decision making and prioritization become less confusing. Through experimentation and introspection, we gain clarity and are no longer filled with doubt. It starts to feel easier when we courageously dive into the unfamiliar, over and over again, and we expand our capacity. With new skills, knowledge, and eventually, wisdom, we become so much more likely to achieve our most meaningful goals.

Remember that *capacity zone*? It is essential to realize that our capacity zone relates to a particular *point in time*. It is our capacity zone as of *now*. If we think of our capacity as static, that would mean that we have stopped growing and that we are indeed getting old. If we instead take on the perspective that we *gain capacity by doing*, and by being willing to have new experiences, we can actually "grow closer" to achieving our big goals and remain youthful.

In this section we will explore specific ways to gain awareness and keep implementing ways that truly support us and our goals. When we look at it this way, we empower ourselves by purposefully creating our path of growth. We choose projects and action steps that will help us grow into that future self and that have the capacity to achieve the big dream!

When we connect the steps we commit to today and this week to how we will grow our capacity to achieve our most meaningful goals, we empower ourselves.

An added bonus with such a purposeful approach is that often when we direct our attention and get into action, "the universe provides." When we have a clear goal and a path, we are so much more likely to accept these serendipitous offerings. We are more likely to see the ways that we are supported and we can acknowledge when "just what we needed" shows up on our path.

Regular Reflection/Introspection

An essential and practical way to be deliberate about our use of time is to reflect regularly and plan frequently. That is how we gain insights and awareness about what works for us personally. Through our choices, we empower ourselves to truly live *our* lives, in alignment with our values, dreams, and ambitions.

It's important to re-energize our goals, to reconnect to what helps us go from stuck to re-inspired, and to pursue our project with new resources and with new perspectives. We can access multiple empowering perspectives and learn tools that help us move forward, even when we come up against obstacles—whether external or internal—through engaging activities where we tap into our wisdom (all that experience we do have!). The trick is to find what's blocking us and then use techniques to determine what the next right step is. We'll get to discover how a growth mindset can free us as well as empower us. We'll take home a ritual that will help us continually course-correct so that we know we are aligned with our bigger goals, values, and dreams.

The way we get that clarity is to incorporate times in our schedule to step away from *doing* and check in with ourselves. We take a moment to feel into how it is going and what we need.

"Catch Yourself" Soon and Often

You might assume that as a Time Management Coach, I am always fully focused, crystal clear on my priorities, and on track. I hate to disappoint . . . but I believe that is an unachievable goal. With the demanding and ever-changing circumstances and complexity of our lives, it is in fact completely normal to get distracted, confused, and sometimes overwhelmed. That comes with the choice of living at the edge of our comfort zone and always exploring what else we are capable of.

If, at a time when we feel stressed, we take a moment to consider what *specifically* is causing the friction, then we can make a deliberate choice about how we show up in that situation. With each such deliberate choice, we empower ourselves.

One day I felt a bit overwhelmed and unfocused. I'd accumulated lots of tasks (stickies) and it felt like I was a bit behind in nearly all aspects. Prior to that, I had allowed myself to be fully focused on one top priority during a holiday: being fully present with my family. As I re-engaged, I almost immediately felt overwhelmed. There was so much to catch up on! As I stopped for a moment to consider what I was doing, I realized that it was a matter of giving my planning session the focus it deserved. I had gotten into *doing* mode before being clear about my true priorities and had not been realistic about my weekly and daily plans. I felt anxious about what I might be missing that was hiding in that pile of tasks. I was busy, but working without a sense that I was making any significant progress on anything of significance.

This is one example of when we need to remind ourselves to *pause*. When we feel stress levels or confusion rise, it's time to stop doing. We are better off unlatching from action mode for a moment to *zoom out* to see the bigger picture. It will likely feel counterintuitive to stop doing when there is so much to do and the to-do list seems to be growing faster than we can check things off. However, staying in this "crazed" mode will require a lot of energy, and while we might get some things checked off our list, we will probably feel like we are barely making a dent. It's time to raise our gaze out of the trees so that we can better see the forest.

Sometimes we end up wasting time mindlessly. For example, many people, me included, can get lured down social media rabbit holes and find ourselves having wasted precious time mindlessly scrolling the internet. If you, like I, want to break such a habit, you might want to try this: In a moment of clarity, make a conscious choice about what you want and don't want. I might decide I don't want to get lost down social media rabbit holes, and that I want to replace that habit by taking a couple of deep breaths and asking myself what I really want. Then, any time I find myself (in autopilot) lost in a scroll, I commit myself to pause, take a breath, and then make a deliberate choice.

Beware of Shoulds

It is essential to check in with ourselves and really listen to our emotions because they will affect our ability to focus and make empowered choices. When we think we *should* be a certain way—we *should* already be more skilled than we are, we *should* be stronger, smarter, more capable, we should, well . . . whatever it is—there is probably a message in there to get curious and listen to, but not let it run our lives. Often these "shoulds" are rooted in beliefs that we adopted when we were much younger, when we had less trust in our inner wisdom and more trust in what the grownups around us were saying and what society rewarded us for. Somewhere along the line, we concluded that we would more readily be accepted if we acted a certain way, and dismissed other options. We concluded that being successful looked a certain way, and we were supposed to approach life according to that externally imposed definition of success. We tried to be "good enough" by working hard, pushing through, and enduring. Success became what we saw in magazines: a skinny body, lots of possessions, a well-paid job, and the power that came with lots of responsibilities. Success meant that we were popular, cool, pretty, and "had it all together." Perhaps you, like I, succeeded in *seeming* successful . . . and got lost in what you were actually aiming for—what was deeply meaningful to you.

I bring this up again here because, as we shift into reflection mode, there's a big chance those "shoulds" will rear their ugly head again. We want to make sure we make more deliberate decisions, instead of blindly trying to live up to any imposed shoulds.

Use that Zoom Feature

Like so many things in life, we need to learn to live with paradoxes—situations when we need to hold multiple seemingly contradictory perspectives—see the truth and validity of multiple aspects.

As we discussed in Planning versus Doing modes, one such paradox is the ability to "zoom out" and be aware of a bigger perspective: What do I want long term? What would I want if any current constraints were lifted/dealt with? What matters in my life overall? We also have to be able to zoom in and focus on the task at hand—on what we can do right now, where specifically to start, and how to get into action. Magic happens when we can invite both zoom out and zoom in, and have them inform each other about our action today, what we accomplish as a result, and how that relates to our bigger-picture priorities.

One way to zoom out to get a broader perspective of our situation is to view it through the lens of our core values. Just like Mary noticed that her value of *respect* was not being honored, by zooming out, we can get clarity about what is actually bothering us in a situation and find a more empowered approach. We zoom back in when we apply that awareness to a particular action or interaction.

When we are about to do something scary or overwhelming, it can help to zoom out and reconnect with our bigger goal and our intention—our why. Once we connect with the energy and inspiration of our intention, we can zoom in to apply that energy to the task at hand, knowing that we are doing the hard thing for all the right reasons.

Retrospect and Plan—In Practice

As we move through our days, months, and years, we have many opportunities to reflect and adapt. For each broader time frame, we zoom out a little more to check in on our long-term goals and to what extent we are honoring our intentions.

In summary, the time horizons and type of reflections I propose are:

1. Mini reflection at the end of each day, then plan the next day

2. Slightly deeper reflection at the end of each week, then plan the next week

3. More extensive reflection at the end of each month, then plan the coming month, making sure to refer to our intention statements and bigger goals

4. Zoom out even more when doing a seasonal reflection, checking on our progress of our yearly goals and commitments, and planning the upcoming season

5. Broader reflection still at the end of each year, checking our trajectory and overall direction in life, then choosing key initiatives for the coming year

The benefit of putting in the work to reflect and plan is that we can then be truly present with what we are doing. On a daily basis, when in action mode, we can trust that what is exactly in front of us—our committed action for the day—is exactly where we want to put our attention and direct our energy. We don't need to second-guess ourselves or get distracted by *all* that there is to do eventually.

Daily Reflect and Plan

We cannot manage time, but we can manage our attention. One way we can do that is to start our day before we get into action, by being deliberate with where we put our attention.

Take a moment—and it can really be just a few minutes—each morning and decide what is truly most important today. Before you dive into doing mode, take a broader view of what's actually essential that you accomplish today. Be specific and realistic. It might mean you need to set/reset some expectations with yourself, or with others. After all, you only have so many hours in the day just like everyone else.

Try it. Take a moment each morning to decide where you will put your attention, *Then* get into action. Not only does it help us create a more sane pace, but it makes it so much more likely that we'll feel a sense of accomplishment at the end of the day. We will actually have given our time and energy to something that feels important.

Weekly Reflect and Plan

At the end of each week is a great time to check in on how we did. What worked, what didn't? What got in our way? What did we learn?

If we are diligent about doing a weekly reflection and allow our insights to inform how we plan the next week, we will never go "off track" for very long. Take a moment toward the end of each week to check in, recommit to your goals, and plan the upcoming week.

Monthly Reflect and Plan

A new month! Another great opportunity to pause, to stop "doing" for a moment, and be intentional as we plan our upcoming month.

As a way to empower ourselves and set ourselves up for success (our individual definition of course!), I suggest we look back on our prior month and acknowledge:

- What have I accomplished (even partially)?
- What major hurdles have I dealt with?
- What have I learned?
- What are my insights?

Plan this brand-new month! Informed by your reflection and insights, reconnect with your intentions and key projects.

Some questions you might ask yourself as you reflect on your month:

- What am I proud of accomplishing? What helped me succeed with that?
- What do I want to do differently?
- What's most important in my life right now? What do I choose to give my time to this coming month?
- At the end of *this* new month, what will I be able to acknowledge as done?

Pause in this deliberate way and give yourself a time-vestibule—a moment to arrive from wherever you've just been, a chance to look yourself in the mirror, straighten yourself out, and, as you open the door into your next visit with time, be ready to fully engage.

Seasonally and Yearly Reflect and Plan

The next broader perspective of reflecting and planning that I recommend is every three months. You may choose to do this quarterly, but I much prefer dividing up the year into seasons. Since each season has a different "mode" and focus, I find it useful to let nature and traditions inform me as I plan my seasons.

Here in the northern hemisphere, I consider the winter months to be December until February, spring the months of March, April, and May, summer from June through August, and fall taking us from September to the end of November.

Winter season includes holidays, shifting from old year to new year, and likely more indoor time. For our *yearly* planning (mid-winter in the northern hemisphere), it can be useful and fun to do a little "time travel": Imagine you are getting ready to head out to a New Year's party at the end of ***next*** year. You've suited up in your best glitter and glam, a bottle of chilled bubbly in hand. A brand-new year is *just* around the corner—tomorrow! During your ride to the party (a COVID-safe one of course), you reflect back on your most proud achievements of the past year. What will you celebrate?

We can use such time travel to connect with an imagined future state, and let that inform how we spend our time. When we connect emotionally with that desired future, we can energize our commitment to act. By getting into aligned action, we empower ourselves to use our time for meaningful activities.

Spring is bright and makes it easier (for most) to get traction and go full speed ahead. We can leverage the energy of the natural cycle of growth that is all around us and the longer and lighter days.

Summer might mean more time with friends, the kids out of school, longer evenings, perhaps a vacation, or staycation, maybe a bit of a slowdown in areas of (our) business. It can be harder to keep our attention on business initiatives when all we want to do is play! It can be useful to consider how we will continue to make progress and keep the momentum we've created so far this year, even as we allow more time for summer play.

Fall provides some of the energy of a new year. The engines are revving, schools have started, businesses are fully back in full swing, and the end of the year suddenly seems closer. It's time to refocus on our most important goals for the year and finish strong. But before you kick into gear, consider: Where are you headed?

Finding Your Very Personal How

You and I might have a similar *why* (intention) and *what* (action plan), but might choose a very different *how* in our approach to reaching our goals.

Let's say that you and I have both determined that: As a marketing manager of our business (role), we want to be visible and easily found by our ideal clients (goal), so that we can serve more people with our services (intention). One initiative we have chosen to pursue is to increase our social media presence and a specific action might be to engage on a chosen social media platform. Yet, we might have a very different approach to *how* we do that. One of us might create a very detailed plan, create all the posts upfront, and schedule them to go out multiple times each week. Another might make a commitment to share content and connect on social media twice a week, but allow the actual content to be more organic and "in the moment." Both these approaches would point to that same intention, but allow for the preferences and personality of the person completing the action.

As a new business owner, a new parent, or perhaps a person new in your career, you might not know yet what fits you. Great news: The way to discover is by experimentation and reflection. You can get into action now, before you are *quite* ready, and learn from doing.

WE CAN'T MANAGE TIME, BUT . . .

As mentioned before, rather than thinking that we can manage time, it is much more powerful to reflect on how we can manage our *attention*, our *energy*, and ours as well as others' *expectations*. These three "lenses" can be very useful as we reflect and plan our next timeframe, be it a day, a week, a month, or even a bigger perspective like a decade, or our lifetime.

What we manage is *not* time. What we manage is at deeper levels. If we learn to unpack and inspect expectations, to diligently direct our attention and deliberately manage our energy, the way we *experience time* will be enriched and deeply meaningful.

If I notice that I'm feeling stressed or agitated due to a growing to-do list, I can use these perspectives to assess what is off, and what adjustments to make in order to feel like I am realigned and setting myself up to succeed.

Here are a few questions to guide this reflection:

Attention

- Is my attention narrow or broad? What might I notice if I shift perspective?
- Am I focusing on the difficulties of my situation, or the possibilities that might be available?
- Am I focused on my insanely long never-ending to-do list, or on the progress I am actually making—the growing of my Done list?

- Where do I choose to put my attention right now? What does that mean about other priorities? How will I manage everything that is competing for my attention?

Energy

- To what am I currently giving my energy (thoughts, people, tasks)? How does that align with where I *want* to invest my energy?

- Am I giving energy to thoughts about worst-case scenarios or investing my energy in actually moving forward one step at a time?

- Is my energy scattered by dibble-dabbling, or am I deliberately giving it to the one task at hand?

- What is my energy level, and how can I refuel?

- How am I leveraging masculine, feminine, and child energies? What qualities would serve me if I added more?

Expectations

- What are the expectations I have of myself related to my current workload? Are they realistic, fair, and aligned with my values?

- What expectations am I trying to live up to? Do they make sense?

- What do I need to do to communicate my needs and set expectations with others?

The Fundamentals of Self-Care

As part of our reflection, it's important to consider to what extent we have taken care of ourselves. Because what capacity do we have to take care of all our responsibilities if we don't take care of ourselves? During the time period we are considering, how did you care for your physical, emotional, mental, and spiritual well-being?

Self-care does not necessarily mean pampering or making some extraordinary or fancy arrangements. Self-care can be saying "no" to a night out because we need to rest. It can mean going for a run at lunch instead of hanging out with colleagues, to get out of our heads and energize our bodies. It might mean blocking time on our calendar to step away from our desk, even for five minutes, and do a couple of stretches, even when our to-do list is long and we have back-to-back meetings on our calendar. It requires that we keep bringing in our overall intentions for sustainable and healthy living and apply them to our daily choices.

Self-care can be making the appointment for our mammogram, cleaning our office, or throwing away those bras that don't fit quite right.

Self-care can mean that we do what energizes us or plug the ways our energy is drained. Self-care can mean that we set aside time and put ourselves on our calendar before it is filled with demands from others. Self-care can mean that, in addition to giving our attention to others' well-being, we also prioritize our own well-being today and in the future.

Keep it Fresh, Keep it Going

There are an infinite number of approaches we can use to reflect and gain insight into what is working for us, and what's not. To keep this aspect of your practice energized and full of curiosity, make sure you mix it up and keep looking for inspiring ways to reflect. You'll become more and more self-aware and subsequently make more informed and deliberate choices about where you invest your precious attention and energy, and your time. Below are some ideas.

Journaling

When things don't go the way we plan, it's especially important to reflect. Do some free-form journaling to find nuance not only about what you got done, but as a way to tap into more soulful aspects of the reflection. Reflect about the quality of being, what values you are honoring, how you've felt, your sense of feeling connected, etc.

Using Metaphor

I did a visualization with one of my coaches and realized that when I felt overworked, I had this sense of being pulled in all directions, and each direction was tense like a tightened rubber band. Just a little stronger pull, and the metaphorical rubber band would either break or sharply snap back at me. Whenever I applied myself and leaned in to focus on one aspect, another part would get even tighter. Then my coach asked what I would like to *replace* this metaphor with. I almost instantly envisioned a Buddha statue. This Buddha was golden, smiling, and had a substantial weight to it. I realized that I longed for the sense of feeling centered and grounded. My Buddha had multiple arms softly reaching out to support others. Each arm had a soft bend in the elbow and reaching out would never take him off his center or agitate his balance. I considered how that way of being could support me, how that way of reaching out and being of service to others without overextending myself could help me stay centered. Since then, any time I notice that feeling of rubber bands overextending, I remind myself of these visuals and can choose to tap into the centered and more balanced energy of my inner golden Buddha.

I took a client of mine through the same visualization at a time when she felt stuck in her life. When asked what it felt like, the metaphor that showed up for her was that she felt as if her whole body was stuck in a thick mud and she could not move. After feeling into that and then getting curious about what she might want to replace the metaphor with, she realized that the mud was malleable and she could actually use it to shape it into what she actually wanted. She could use whatever she was stuck in to create something new in her life. When applied back to her life, she realized that, although she felt stuck in her role at work, she could actually shape some aspects of her role into what she really wanted.

Talk to Someone

It can be hard to see our own tendencies. The way we approach things and see the world might actually be what gets in our way, without us being aware of it. One way to broaden our perspective and tap into our own resourcefulness is to gather with someone you trust and debrief the week or month together. We tend to see ourselves more clearly when we have that external support. It may be a close friend who is committed to being there for your continued growth. It might be a mentor who is invested in your success. Or it might be a coach you hire to support you in pursuing this radical act of living your life to its fullest. Whoever you recruit, look for someone who believes in your capacity to grow, someone who is not judgmental and is willing to honor your intentions.

If Your Body Could Talk

Remember the sense of alignment that we can feel in our body when we get a clear "yes" from our mind, heart, and gut? Did you know that we actually have three brains? We hold a lot of our "intelligence" in our head-brain, sure, but we also have a sense of knowing in our gut and in our heart. In fact, there are more impulses going *from* our heart *to* our brain than the other way around, and the gut is often called our second brain because its network of neurons has more nerve cells than the spinal cord or our (head) brain.

There is so much intelligence in our bodies. Beyond our brain, gut, and heart, all of our body parts hold our memories, our beliefs, and our soul's longing. We might clench our jaw when we are stressed, hold tension in our stomach when we are worried, and restrict our breath when we are afraid. What if our legs could speak? What would they say? I actually explored that once in a workshop and when I really listened, I discovered that my legs were tired of always working hard and getting me places, always doing the leg work (ha!). They wanted to have some fun too—to dance, be silly, move without a destination, just for the fun of it. That revealed a truth, or tendency, in my life. I tend to be very driven and work toward goals and deadlines to make things happen. And yet, I love and long for more playfulness and lightness along the way. I paused to consider, "How could I add some of that (longing) in my daily life, starting right now?" I realized that I dreaded creating my budget for the year. Rather than forcing myself to work it out in a spreadsheet, I got my crayons out and drew my budget! Later on I did enter it into a spreadsheet, but the playfulness of using crayons really helped me get through this task that I dreaded.

When we listen in for these more subtle layers of longing in our body and honor them, we can center ourselves and be more present with what is. It can be as simple as focusing on your breath, paying attention to sensations in your body, noticing tension, and getting curious about how emotions sit in your body.

I want you to keep your process fresh by finding ways to make the reflections varied and fun. Rather than just going through the motions and doing your reflections for the sake of getting them done, I hope you can keep it interesting.

For more ideas about fresh ways to reflect, visit: www.TimeAlchemyResources.com.

PART 6

PUTTING IT ALL TOGETHER

"Real change, enduring change, happens one step at a time."

– Ruth Bader Ginsburg

Go Easy/Fragile Beginnings

As we embark on the path of achieving our big dreams, it's important to have self-compassion. It's easy to have high expectations and be disappointed if we don't make significant progress right off the bat. We might feel like we are "failing" at first when we are really learning and growing.

In the fragile beginnings of a new endeavor, it is especially important to consider how we can set ourselves up for success. Once we have claimed a few small successes, our commitment "muscles" get stronger, and we can take more courageous steps toward our goals. Once we have gotten a little traction, we might become even more committed to our goals. With consistent action over time, we can step it up a bit and stretch our boundaries more fully. It's important to realize that we need to keep bringing ourselves to that growing edge, and that is usually not entirely comfortable. Any time we fear looking incapable, making a mess, or making a fool of ourselves, we can remind ourselves to have a growth mindset. We can acknowledge that we are brave enough to be a work-in-progress, and aim to always be growing.

I used to carefully hide my insecurities and try to put up a polished and capable front in pretty much everything I did, but over time I've realized that being a work-in-progress is something to be proud of. When you dare to take on projects or tasks that you are not sure will succeed, true growth can happen. You will likely, like I, fall back into worrying about how you will be judged by your peers, your spouse, your neighbors. Each time that happens we need to bring our attention back to our work-in-progress mindset, and keep building the muscle for taking these moderate risks.

We can start with smaller challenges. Remind yourself, and tell others that, "This is my next step, not the be-all-end-all. I don't know for sure if it will work, but if it does, I believe it will make a difference. If it doesn't, it is sure to provide insight and experience."

On days when we don't complete all that we committed to, or don't feel very successful around our action, we need to give ourselves a break—breathe, pause. Rather than beating ourselves up for it, we can get curious and consider what we are learning. We might want to adjust the size of the action steps. We might realize that there was a preparatory step that had to happen before *this* action could be completed. Great! We can now apply what we learned to the next "next step."

Recruit Your Team of Allies

As we courageously go after our dreams, it is essential to surround ourselves with people who dare to believe in our dream, and who will be there to carry us through the rough patches. It may be only a small number of like-minded, supportive, soul searching, growth-oriented, and courageous beings who will be by our side as we dive into this dynamic exploration. We might team up with a colleague or friend to support each other, brainstorm, and make requests of each other.

When we, as driven professionals, don't achieve what we committed to do, we do not need someone else to wag a finger at us to "hold us accountable." We tend to be tough enough on ourselves.

What we need is compassion and support that help us figure out what we can learn from each experience. This support can come in many forms: a dear friend, a supportive colleague, a coach, or a mentor. Make sure it is someone who courageously believes that you can achieve your dreams!

When we, as people who aim to live a life of integrity, fall short of delivering on a promise, we do *not* need "the stick." What most of us need is someone who will show up to support us in growing from the experience. We are all "work-in-progress" and it's up to us to take a moment to reflect on what we can learn from the lessons life presents.

Often the fear of looking bad or incapable is much bigger in our minds than what others would actually notice, or care about, if we indeed "failed." Once we are ready to go for a bigger goal where more is at stake, we need to make sure we feel supported. Who are the people who will be there for us whether we succeed or stumble? Even a great influencer like Martin Luther King Jr. surrounded himself with very capable people, all leaders in their own right. His impact was possible thanks to many people.

Find a group where everyone is ready to show up for each other and go out and achieve extraordinary things!

I've been able to write this book because my husband has supported me financially, emotionally, and culinarily while writing. At the moment of this writing, I still have not fully understood all the support and different skills that I will need to enlist to get the book into hands and my tools into good use in people's lives. If I was to "go it alone" it would take the rest of my life to learn each of the steps. With qualified support, I can put this book out in much less than a lifetime and then keep working on what I am most passionate about: amplifying the impact of women solopreneurs who want to have a positive impact in the world by offering my skills to them.

Expand Your Capacity through Others

As I went out "on my own," I had no prior experience running an entire company. Not only did I become a coach, as intended, I also had to become an accountant, a marketeer, a CEO, a customer care rep, my own IT support, and so much more. Over the years, I have gradually grown my capacity and have learned lots by doing:

- I've learned how to do meaningful networking, first by awkwardly attending networking events that did not feel genuine, then finding my tribe and building connections with people I really want on my team.

- I've learned how to create and deliver impactful programs through trial and error. Some were pilot programs that didn't stick, but that helped me create a better program next time.

- Through speaking and writing, I've grown my capacity to communicate ideas in a way that is useful to others (I hope you agree!), not always "nailing it" but learning and fine-tuning with each experience by daring to put my voice out there and listen to the responses.

None of that happened overnight. Rather, it required me to take one wobbly, yet deliberate step after the other.

Pressing "publish" for my very first blog post was definitely a "feel the fear and do it anyway" moment. It felt like a leap into unknown and scary territory. Nothing "bad" happened, and then I took the next step: writing my next post. Then the next. Step by step, I learned to become a writer. Interaction by interaction I gained confidence that I could serve by conveying my message.

At this point, as I look at my situation from the "capacity zone" perspective, I am more willing to take support from others. I'm willing to tap into the skill and knowledge of other business owners. I've become aware and have consciously decided which capacities I am *actually* interested in acquiring versus those I'll gladly get help with.

Since my mission in this life is not to become a publisher or get a grip on the book industry, I stay in my brilliance and engage in activities that continue to increase it. It includes taking big, fluffy concepts and theories and make them accessible in people's very real daily lives, supporting as many people as possible in living a life of choice.

In the last few years, I have learned more about domains, DNS records, and APIs than I ever wanted to know (although I still don't know what all those acronyms stand for!). In hindsight, I wish I had taken support to get that all set up for me. If I had asked myself at the time, "Do I *want* to grow my capacity of maintaining the backend of my website?" I would likely have answered "no" and could have deliberately given my attention to other aspects of my business. If I had hired help for what was not in my wheelhouse, or what I even aspired to have in my wheelhouse, I would have built my business *much* faster and with less frustration. I can see now that what I expected of myself, as a solopreneur, was to prove that I could do it *all*.

An Empowered Future

At a future state, your capacity zone has grown and now overlaps *almost* completely with the cloud shape labeled "Where your dreams come true." In addition, *someone else's* capacity zone covers the remaining piece of what's required to fully accomplish your dream.

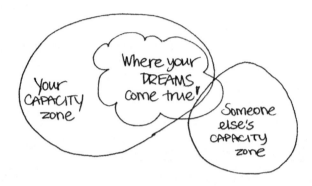

> • What skills, knowledge, or capacity, is required, but is not something you truly want to get good at?

Who Will You Recruit? Who's on Your Team?

There is immense power in having an accountability partner, a group, or an individual who will hold us to what we promised—not in an authoritative finger-wagging way, but as a support that will help us stick to what we have decided is important to us. The only way I believe we can fail is when we ignore what doesn't work, when we don't learn from it, and instead keep chugging along in exactly the same way. The only failure is when we fail to reflect and learn from our experiments. Having an accountability appointment is powerful because we will need to own up to why we did not deliver on our promise, and most of us are people with integrity. We want to stand by our word, sometimes more to others than to ourselves. Having to "fess up" to not delivering on our commitment somewhat publicly—even if only with one other person—

makes it harder to shove it under the rug and pretend it never happened. How many missed commitment dust balls do you have under your rug? Isn't it time to do a deep cleaning and stop sweeping them under there? Shake out that rug and clean the floor underneath.

- Who do you need on your support team?

Accountability can sound harsh, as if someone else—our accountability partner—will sternly demand that we report back that we did *everything* we committed to doing. If we didn't, we failed to live up to our word.

But we all know that "life happens" and our plans cannot always work out. As a matter of fact, they often don't. Circumstances change. Tasks are more complex or daunting than we anticipated. We plan way too optimistically, telling ourselves "I will do it *all* this week." Then we don't finish. We procrastinate. We get disappointed in ourselves. We don't need anybody else's whip to come down on us; most of us are hard enough on ourselves. We see ourselves as driven, ambitious, disciplined. We don't want to be babysat and micromanaged. What we do long for is support, a little comradery, and a sense that "I'm not alone in this." That would be really nice!

We do not need to go at it alone and we are even unlikely to make a big impact if we isolate ourselves. Let's put our dream and our core skills and passion at the center, and then surround ourselves with people who have complementary dreams, who have a similar "big picture" goal, and start collaborating in order to make it come true.

What's Possible from Here

Lifelong Explorations

As mentioned many times over by now, I believe it's a good thing that we will never be "done."

As lifelong learners, there is so much we know, yet there is so much to learn. The more we know, the more we realize how little we know. I have provided practical and versatile tools that can be used again and again. My intent was to give you a starting place that is meant to be adjusted based on your regular reflection and daily deliberate choices.

I hope you are convinced to try, yet do not take my word for it. My approach has supported hundreds of people with very different circumstances, but you need to see for yourself. Keep the main three principles:

1. Define your inspired intentions.

2. Determine the next aligned action.

3. Adopt the practice of ever-evolving experimentation, and allow the rest to be shaped in a way that fits you.

We each get to define "success" for us personally and, even so, it is a moving target. Even if we define a really big goal and aim to reach it, when we have been on our mission for a while and approach the goal, we are likely to be better informed. We might fine-tune or perhaps change the goal significantly. Like that boat heading over the Atlantic toward Portugal, we might change course on purpose, because Morocco sounds pretty intriguing after all.

In summary, attitudes that will support you as you experiment your way to your individual approach include:

- Commit to showing up with an open mind, with an appetite for learning, with courage in doing something that feels like a stretch.

- Commit to being present in the moment, to experiencing your days, not letting them go by in auto-pilot mode.

- Commit to making choices and getting into action even when you don't quite know the end result. Start implementing now, even if you don't quite know your overall life's purpose or how you are going to achieve it.

- Commit to getting into action even when you don't *feel like it*. Connect to your bigger *why* of those tasks, and get into action "even though . . . "

- Commit to ongoing exploration about what it means to you to live a *rich* life.

We can't know exactly what we *will* find meaningful and inspiring in a few years, but we can add meaning and richness to our daily experiences, starting now.

Imagine living your life—*this* one—hour by hour and day by day, moment by moment—in a way that feels fulfilling and deeply satisfying to your soul. It takes dedication and continuous recommitment, and I have shown you how. It is not easy but, oh, *such* a good investment. Since you're living anyway, why not live your most engaged and meaningful life? I'm convinced that you can reach the end of your life with a sense of truly having lived *your* life to its *fullest*. But you need to start now and do what you can to avoid regrets. That way you will know that you really gave it your best shot. What would it be worth to you to reflect back on your life and know that, "Yes, I really lived a life true to myself, not the one that was expected of me. I went for my dreams, lived my potential."?

Yes, that is what is at stake here: your life.

And, really, managing your time is a way to manage your life.

I trust that you can now see how the practices and principles of this book will serve as the foundation as you build your very own, unique time management approach—one you allow to organically take shape based on your actual experiences and preferences, that allows a sprinkle of lightness and a good dose of curiosity as you test out what actually supports you in doing more of what matters with your time.

I hope you stop trying to "manage your time" and instead regularly assess and adjust your attention, your expectations, and how you manage your energy. Once you do this, and dare to go for your dreams, you empower yourself to create a truly rich existence of time in your daily life. Now *that* is how we become Time Alchemists!

Keep Discovering

I wish you continued appetite for life, always savoring what you are currently experiencing and remaining curious about what else life has to offer. Keep exploring.

From now on, I hope you get curious whenever something is not working, and get really curious about what *could* work. Then try that; make it a new experiment. The only way it will fail is if you fail to learn and grow from it.

My hope is that you find ways to be fully present in the process, more invested in experiencing the journey of your life than in reaching particular goals. I hope you aim to live a daily inspired and rich life, the kind of life you want to look back at and say, "Oh yeah, that was really *my* life, and did I ever live it fully!"

I'd be delighted if these explorations have helped you discover and more fully own your unique gifts, and fully live *your* life. We each have a unique set of qualities, ambitions, and quirks that can serve a specific need in the world. Keep stretching into your next growing edge and fully experience this one precious life.

There *is* an urgency, because life *is* passing us by. If we don't show up to experience our days, don't turn within and listen for what most matters, if we don't allow our dreams to expand and take form and get shared in the world, we will just "get by," live on auto-pilot, live our life ruled by external expectations, and end up missing "the point" of this one unique and precious life. Don't die with your soul's longing unexpressed.

Living a deeply meaningful life is a journey. It will sometimes be bumpy, sometimes full of obstacles but, oh, what a rich experience. We enrich ourselves by fully participating in those experiences. We become wiser, more fulfilled, and more fully ourselves as we stretch our comfort zone and grow our capacity zone.

During your journey, know that:

- You are worthy.
- You are needed.
- You are enough.

Addendum: Common Dilemmas

So, how do these principles and practices hold up, even in challenging situations?

If you have doubts about how you can implement the approach that has been presented in this book, congratulations! It points to two good insights:

1. The fact that you notice your doubts means a level of self-awareness—yay! Now you can do something about it!

2. The other good news is that, by questioning the approach, you likely have a healthy level of skepticism and, hopefully, a willingness to test how you might apply and adjust for your preferences and your particular situation. Both are great first steps in shaping an approach that truly works for you.

This work can be challenging as we come up against multiple dilemmas in this complex world of ours. As the complex beings we are, we are also likely to come up against parts of ourselves (doubts, frustration, impatience) that get in our way. Any time we face a dilemma, feel stuck, or perhaps feel deflated, it's useful to consider different perspectives as a way to unpack our view of the situation and thereby get access to more potential ways forward.

Once you have acknowledged a dilemma (challenge, obstacle, resistance . . .), you are in a position to either override it and push through, or you can inquire within and make deliberate choices about what to do next.

I want to remind you that when we deal with our different time dilemmas, rather than trying to "manage time," we are better off using the "lenses" that direct us to what we *can* manage, namely our *attention, energy,* and *expectations.* Let's explore how to apply that by spotlighting some common dilemmas and hopefully help you get traction.

In a broad perspective, here are examples of how we can use these lenses to inquire. No matter what the challenge, here are some ways to consider:

- What **energy** do you need more of, the masculine (strategy, discipline, tactics), the feminine (patience, allowing, compassion), or the child (play, experimentation, curiosity)?

- Where is **energy** stuck or draining? How are you recharging your energy and finding flow?

- Where are you putting your **attention**—mentally, physically, emotionally, spiritually?

- Is your **attention** on what's working or on what's not? Is it on your current lack or on the ways you are growing?

- What **expectations** do you have of yourself regarding just how much you're "supposed to accomplish"? What's considered success, or what's good enough?

- What external **expectations** are you trying to live up to—generally, specifically?

If you and I were actually sitting across from each other, this unpacking would obviously be very specific to you and your situation. There are so many possible routes of exploration. Nevertheless, I hope the below explorations of common scenarios will help you discover some potential next steps.

I am so crazy busy that I can't even think beyond today, let alone dream about some ideal state in the future.

I get it and you are not alone! This is such a common dilemma. In our driven society and with the intense demands of our careers, business, and/or families, it can feel hard enough to keep our noses above water. When we are that busy, of course we stay action oriented. How else would we ever get ahead enough to get a breather? I think it is a very dangerous and unsustainable approach, and being the driven optimists we are, we think that "next week will be better," but it rarely it is.

What I suggest you consider in this situation is, what trajectory are you on? If you continue like this for another year—or five, or twenty—where will it take you? How will your body, your friendships, your family, your career, your community be better or worse off? Once you've spent some time envisioning this future state, consider if that is what you truly want to aim for.

It's been so long since I allowed myself to dream, I don't even know what I want anymore.

Life can seem to take on a life of its own and we end up really busy just getting by. This is very common. Time seems to fly by and we are so busy that we barely have time to care for our basic wants and needs, let alone the time to dream.

If you were sitting across from me now, I would probably start by asking you to take a deep breath. Take a moment to arrive, right here and now. We might then explore this dilemma through the lens of energy. In this small space of time, right here, right now, try to recall an activity that you loved to do as a child, or at an earlier time in your life. In your mind's eye, see yourself back in that situation and feel into the experience. How does the activity energize you or light you up? Now, imagine yourself in the future engaging in a similar activity. See yourself in action and notice any positive effect on your being. Make a mental note of any insights from that, and come back to here and now.

How was that? What insights did you get from this very brief visualization? What, specifically, was enjoyable about either your past or your imagined future experience?

This kind of time travel (remembering the past and envisioning the future) is always available to us. Within minutes, we can remind ourselves about what energizes us, what makes us come alive. Even small "trips" like that will start to build your dreaming "muscle" and energize you ever so slightly.

Now, go add that insight to one of your intention statements, and think of one *tiny thing* you can do this week to honor that dream. If you used to love to play the piano and remembered how much you enjoy listening, perhaps commit to listening to your favorite piano piece on your lunch break. If you reconnect with your love of traveling and the way it opens your mind, think of one way you can add a new place and sense of adventure in your day.

I know what I want but I'm a master procrastinator! How do I get focused and into action?

Of all the time management dilemmas I hear about, this is clearly the most common. Some of us are occasional procrastinators, some are "pros." Either way, it can be hard to overcome, especially if it has become a habit to allow ourselves to avoid certain tasks.

The most obvious choice would be to explore this dilemma through the lens of attention, since we want to manage our attention toward what we have committed to, rather than what happens to pull our attention away in the moment. Although that would very likely provide insight, I'd like to share how you might use a less obvious choice of exploration: energy.

Energy management can help us overcome procrastination if we take a moment to remember the bigger *why* for this task—the reason we prioritized it in the first place. How will this task provide an outcome that is likely to take us closer to our goal or intention? Assuming you have clarified a truly inspiring intention for yourself, connecting back to that might be enough of a "pull" to get you over the hump and into action. Also, make sure to break down any large, looming tasks you really find hard into something less intimidating and more doable. Getting into action creates momentum and makes *more* energy available to you.

If that doesn't quite do it, here is something useful to understand about our brains: As you might know, neural pathways are created as a result of our behavior and our brain saves energy by taking the route of least resistance, using the most engrained and frequently used paths. It actually takes significant mental effort to redirect away from habitual behavior toward doing something that is new, requires analytical thinking, or is otherwise energy consuming for the brain. We can think of it as "limbic friction" (a term coined by Andrew Huberman). It can be really helpful to expect the first ten minutes or so of a demanding task to be difficult, due to this friction.

To get yourself into action on a demanding task, try giving yourself a start-up "timebox": Decide on a short time frame (like ten minutes). Commit to give your full attention to the task and do as much as you can during that time. After the ten minutes, you may make a new choice about where to direct your attention, but chances are you have overcome the "limbic friction" by then and can take on the next task with less resistance.

In addition, imagine the energy that will be freed once you are done! Rather than wasting energy avoiding the task over and over and over, take the more energy-efficient approach and *just do it*, thereby benefitting from the energy boost you will get by having it *be done!*

My days are extremely unpredictable and others' demands determine my days. I really don't have control of my time.

Many roles can seem so all-consuming that we feel like we have very little choice about how we use our time. You might be parenting, teaching, or caretaking. You might have a service-oriented profession or an extremely volatile work situation. Any of those scenarios can leave us feeling like we are at the mercy of what others need hour by hour, or of what they demand from us minute by minute. Fortunately, we have a lot to work with when it comes to our *experience* of time. We can make choices about *how* we show up for such demanding work.

For this dilemma, I'd like to illustrate a way to work with expectations by sharing a brief story. Catherine, a client of mine, was a mid-level manager in a service organization. She managed a team of five, was a key contributor on multiple broad company initiatives, and was also dealing with especially gnarly internal service requests. Most days she felt pushed and pulled by the demands of those projects, needs from her team, and impatient internal customers. She felt like she had very little control over her time. After some exploration, she realized she was not setting any boundaries about when she was available and when she was not. She felt like she *had* to be available to her team and her customers and very rarely got undisturbed time to do the deeper work required for her projects. She reminded herself of the importance of her projects and the critical role she played in their success, and realized that some of the other demands were definitely lower priority. She realized that she could set expectations with her team that she would be unavailable during certain hours each (most) days. She communicated with her team, blocked her calendar, and then, when the time came, closed her door and got traction on some of her most important tasks.

Even when we feel like we have no choice, usually we do. If we are willing to truly prioritize and be clear to others about what we need in order to succeed, we can make time for what matters most.

If you are in a similar situation, where you feel like others' demands dictate your time, I recommend you take inventory of all that you feel responsible for (write it all out). Identify the most frustrating or limiting aspect and consider what you actually need that would make it more manageable.

Fill in the blank: "If only_____(desire)." "What I really need is_____." Then, get creative, by yourself or with your colleagues, a coach, or another supportive person in your life. Think of something you can do to make your situation better, then go make requests to others and set expectations accordingly.

I am full of ideas and ambition—I'm multi-passionate! How can I make time for it all?

In my work I have the fortune of working with many driven and ambitious individuals. I love the energy that my multi-passionate friends, colleagues, and clients have! Although that kind of enthusiasm and drive is admirable, sometimes they get in their own way because they start pursuing so many things in parallel that they make little progress on anything. As a result, they feel overwhelmed and a bit disillusioned due to the lack of progress. These same folks, and I'd include myself in this category, tend to be go-getters. Everything seems like a great opportunity. They jump on it, and their plates end up overflowing.

Essentially this is a self-inflicted act of going into overwhelm and, yes, I sometimes end up there too! We are so ambitious that we eagerly say "yes" to too many things, jump on opportunities without considering what we've already committed to, and end up with too many work-in-progress initiatives. Similar to our goal to limit tasks that are work-in-progress, on a macro level, when we have too many larger initiatives in progress, we are less likely to gain significant momentum on any one of them. We end up context switching between our projects without gaining much traction anywhere. We are better off choosing a small number of initiatives that we complete before starting another one.

For most people in this situation it is useful to realize that you can have it all, eventually. To get traction, I recommend looking at larger time buckets and committing to fewer projects that you pursue simultaneously. For example, if you are eager to try out ten new hobbies, or test out five potential new programs in your business, you can decide to pursue two of them in the next month (or longer depending on their size and complexity). During that time you would "park" all other ideas and give the committed initiative your full energy and attention. Eventually you can pursue them all, but for now, of all that you want to create, accomplish, or learn, what smaller number of initiatives do you want to commit to first?

I'm very much a "doer" and all this introspection and planning seems like fluff.

In this action-oriented, achievement-focused, and fast-moving world, it can feel completely counter to our drive to stop doing. I absolutely feel the tendency to get into doing every morning and every beginning of a new week.

If we are constantly and continuously in action mode and don't stop to reflect, we actually miss out on a lot of information that would help us more efficiently get more done! A couple things to consider that can help with this resistance:

1. What time on a daily basis, and day on a weekly basis, am you *most likely* to be able to disconnect from action mode and tune into a more reflective state? For me, it's become clear that when Monday morning rolls around, I am so eager to get into motion that forcing myself to first plan my week feels excruciatingly limiting. Therefore, I've made it a habit to do my weekly reflection + planning last thing on Friday afternoons. On Monday morning I can do a quick fine-tuning and dive right in! For you, it might be different. Perhaps Sunday afternoon is a good quiet time for you to reflect and plan your week.

2. Another tip if you feel eager to just get going is to start with very brief reflect + plan sessions. Start weaving in some amount of reflection and planning in your day. It could be as brief as five minutes every morning to set priorities and five minutes at the end of the day to assess if you are, in fact, heading in the direction of where you want to end up.

As you experience increased self-awareness from such reflection, and a sense of self-empowerment from making deliberate choices aligned with your values and intentions, you might be more willing to give it more attention and go a bit deeper in your reflection each week.

I wish I could just clone myself. Asking for help just creates more work. It's easier to double down and do it myself.

I imagine that you have big ambitions for your life, your career, and perhaps your business. You want to have a big impact. There is lots of work to be done, and you want it done according to your standards. You are truly great at your work, and yet, there is only so much you can fit into a day.

I invite you to take a moment and consider a broader perspective: How much bigger could your ambitions be if you set up a support system that works for you—if you leveraged others' brilliance in getting part of the work done?

Think about this: If you consistently continue to double down and push through to get it *all* done yourself, how sustainable is that? Since there is only one of you and you already have a full plate, how scalable is this approach?

If this is a recurring theme in your life, you are better off doing the very counterintuitive but necessary pause and zoom out to get access to a broader perspective. If you can't get unstuck, find a mentor or coach who can help you see more potential options.

This all sounds hard and like a lot of work. Will it be worth my time and energy?

I hear you. All this introspection and figuring out what actually works for you can seem like hard work. It might be useful to consider the attention and energy you give to the process, to becoming more and more self-aware and self-empowered as an investment. You can also give yourself permission to go at your own pace. Just do some reflection and make one deliberate choice as a result. Perhaps you pause for just a minute at the end of the day to consider, *What worked well for me today? How can I tweak a little something about how I approach tomorrow to make it work better for me?*

You will not be surprised to hear me say that I think it is worth every bit of energy you put into it. That's essentially the point I've been trying to make throughout this book. I think it is worth it because I find life precious and hope you make the most of yours, because the world can benefit from your presence, your skills, and your superpowers.

Here's a little formula that might help you get started. When you feel like it might be too much hard work to do something, take a moment to connect with the positive outcome you hope for as a result of taking that action.

Even though _____ (I don't feel like it or find it hard),

I will _____ (small action step),

Because _____ (intention or expected positive outcome).

Take it for a test run and see if taking some small action gives you energy and perhaps enough momentum to repeat, or take the next small step. Good luck!

I know what I want and I want to make sure I do this right.

When we are pursuing a truly aspirational goal, one that simultaneously excites us and scares the crap out of us, it will feel like a lot is at stake, and we don't want to make mistakes. That is understandable. It can feel awkward and intimidating.

If this is where you find yourself, the most important perspective I'd want to remind you of is that of continuous learning. If we never risk failing, we are likely aiming way too low. Perfectionism is the enemy of progress.

If we wait to take action until we know we will do it perfectly, we are holding ourselves back. Better to stretch our comfort zone by courageously taking on something we deeply care about even though we are unsure we'll succeed. Create experiments with a relatively low risk, go do them, and learn in the process.

Expectation setting can be very helpful in this context. The first time you deliver a new program, consider it "beta" or a "pilot" and ask your participants for constructive feedback about what worked and what didn't. If you are asking for feedback on an article you wrote but feel shy about sharing with the world, take it for a test run with a few trusted colleagues, friends, or clients to hear how it "lands."

Set expectations with others, but most importantly, with yourself. Don't expect perfection when you are just learning. Instead, expect to learn from doing and give yourself a pat on the back for being courageous enough to create something new.

Finally . . .

If you choose to try on any of these approaches to overcome your dilemma, make sure you take some time afterwards to *reflect*, even if only briefly. What worked, what didn't? What are you discovering? What will you try next? This is your journey, your life . . . make it a rich experience filled with curiosity, fascination, and deep fulfillment!

And, I'll leave you with one of my favorite quotes:

"Life should not be a journey to the grave with the intention of arriving safely in a pretty and well-preserved body, but rather to skid in broadside in a cloud of smoke, thoroughly used up, totally worn out, and loudly proclaiming 'Holy smokes, what a ride!'"

– Hunter S. Thompson

For additional resources, worksheets, and ideas, visit:
TimeAlchemyResources.com

AUTHOR BIO
ULRIKA BRÄTTEMARK

As a coach and facilitator, I bring heart-centered solopreneur women together so that we can provide compassionate accountability support and amplify each of our positive impacts on this world.

As a corporate expat, I pull from my agile background and mindset, and leverage my organizational and analytical skills to create offerings so that my clients can benefit from my experience. And I get to keep exploring and creating!

As an expressive arts student and Pippi Longstocking fan, I delight in looking for fresh and unexpected ways to explore how we approach the complexities of life. That way we get to discover new perspectives, integrate paradoxes, and creatively transform obstacles into gifts.

As a wife, I treasure the joint life journey I've experienced with my husband so far, and the adventures still ahead! Not everyone has such a rock in their life.

As a mother of two amazing beings, I am bursting with love and pride and always look forward to my next bear hug and chance to be part of their lives. My children complete me.

As a sister, daughter, friend, and colleague, I cherish the time I've spent in deep conversation and light togetherness because it gives me joy and a sense of meaning and belonging.

As a life enthusiast, I experiment my way through this life journey, always aiming for a truly rich experience, so that my soul becomes both lighter and fuller.

Acknowledgements

As authors do, and I have not been able to fully appreciate this until now, I want to acknowledge the many supporters I've had throughout this process. I get it now. Writing a book is a big undertaking that requires both diligence and a strong support team.

The journey of this book started when I was in corporate, way before I knew that it would lead to a book. To my fellow Agile enthusiasts at Autodesk, thank you for immersing yourselves in the exciting adventures of that very first Scrum team. It was intense and rewarding, and made my approach to life more agile!

To Jeff Daniel, thank you for inviting me to speak about my newly formed Agile Time Management concepts way before I was "ready."

To all my clients, workshop participants, and online followers, I appreciate how you applied parts of this approach to your situation, gave me feedback, and acknowledged its positive impact in your lives.

Thank you Thais Derich for offering a month-long writing challenge, during which I wrote the bulk of this book and started to feel like a writer!

Thank you colleagues, friends, and extended family for words of encouragement along the way. I hope I make you proud.

Thank you Cynthia Gregory and the AUTHOR AUTHOR!! workshop participants for helping me see that I indeed had a fresh perspective and something to contribute.

A *huge* thanks to the woman who helped me make this book a reality: Meredith Eaton (of Eaton Press). You met me exactly where I was (with a huge and messy manuscript) and gently held my feet to the fire as we shaped it all into this book. For a first-time author like myself, the support and guidance you provided was invaluable. You and your brilliant team helped make my dream come true!

And, as the backbone of it all, my family: Thank you for your unconditional cheerleading and wholehearted support. Guido, Ellen, and Emil, I love you to infinity and beyond . . . (you know the rest).

Made in the USA
Middletown, DE
03 April 2022

63535157R00117